Finding a Job

You Can Love

Finding a Job

You Can Love

Ralph T. Mattson and Arthur F. Miller, Jr.

P U B L I S H I N G

P.O. BOX 817 • PHILLIPSBURG • NEW JERSEY 08865-0817

ISBN 0-87552-393-5

CONTENTS

*For we are his workmanship
created in Christ Jesus for
good works, which God prepared
beforehand, that we should walk in
them* (Eph. 2:10 RSV).

INTRODUCTION

EVERY ONCE IN A WHILE, ONE HEARS THE IDEA that life produces occasional "golden opportunities" so special that to ignore them is to play the fool. In my life, this idea came from a diversity of sources, ranging from the stories of King Arthur's court I read as a child to the homespun philosophy of a cleaning lady.

Neither the status of the cleaning lady nor the mythical nature of King Arthur prevented me from believing the idea, so as a child and young adult I assumed that future years would reveal golden opportunities leading to my particular destiny. I never considered much what form it would take, but it certainly was tied to the idea of what I would be when I was on my own, pursuing a career.

Now that I have matured, I can review my years and see that my life has been blessed at certain times with opportunities of such quality that I can admit their being golden. But I have also observed other lives for whom such opportunities seem rare indeed.

This disparity between those who are successful and those who are not has spawned all kinds of popular philosophies, myths, and success techniques. It has helped produce an industry of self-help book publishing aimed at people who are passionate about increasing the frequency of golden opportunities in their lives.

I am not sure whether this volume can be included in that category of publishing. My sense of dignity says no. We are not hawking five secrets of success or ten steps to riches. Yet

7

subsequent chapters are not only written with the aim of helping people to think theologically about the subject of work, but also to equip them in practical ways to find their life's work. In addition, I am somewhat embarrassed to admit that we have a kind of "secret to success" that has had a profound effect on my life, though I am not about to lay claim to any outstanding successes. There may be golden opportunities, but one person's gold is another's dross. And I now see that genuine success has less to do with "golden opportunities" and more to do with what we bring to the ordinary opportunities of life.

Perhaps the best place to start is with the story of an opportunity that came to me as an educator some years ago. I was in the position of putting together a total program of Christian education from early childhood through senior high. Starting from scratch, I was given the freedom to develop what I considered to be ideal education.

From my point of view, the most critical hurdle was not the structuring of administration or the development of curricula. It was not even marketing the program to attract students. For me, the first priority was gathering a dynamic faculty. The possibilities of bringing about an exciting Christian educational community with potential to attract students required the presence of genuine teachers who lived and breathed the stuff of schools.

The problem was how to find these people and identify their gift of teaching. Teaching credentials do not prove that the bearer is a skilled teacher, as any of us who have been through schooling can testify. Recommendations are not dependable. Professors may give rave recommendations to excellent students who will be mediocre teachers. Observation is the best solution, but it is quite impractical with candidates from all over the country.

It was at this time that I met Arthur Miller, who wrote this book with me. He is a consultant who equips corporations to use their human resources to best advantage. To do so, he uses a system called SIMA (System for Identifying Motivated Abilities, described elsewhere in this book) that identifies an individual's "motivated gifts." It enables managers to fit people and projects they are motivated to do.

I asked whether his system could identify which of the candidates were actually motivated to teach. Mr. Miller assured me that SIMA would not only identify teaching abilities, but would also show clearly how each individual should be managed.

We put the candidates through the process. The results were stunning. I was able to know before hiring who was gifted in communicating and influencing students, who wanted to pull teams together, who was motivated to work in tutorials and independent study, who naturally wanted to improve the curriculum, who wanted to follow it exactly, who was able to write a new curriculum, who needed a pat on the back every once in a while, and who shouldn't be bothered. In short, this evaluation process resulted in an exciting faculty with very low turnover, even though we weren't paying fabulous salaries. That was extraordinary.

I then started probing SIMA as a system and put it through long, vigorous testing. I looked at other systems of evaluating people. I compared SIMA results with testing I was already certified to administer. However I approached it, SIMA held true in its accuracy and applicability.

Then I started to use it with young people, especially with those I call Renaissance students. They have honors-level grades, are excellent athletes, and are involved with music, drama, editing yearbooks—they can do anything. They can do anything but do not know what to do with their lives. SIMA was the tool that unraveled their confusion as they saw the pattern of their God-given gifts. Hidden behind their multiple interests was the consistency of a particular way of working and playing SIMA could help them choose educational and career options to pursue, confident of the supporting evidence. SIMA did not make decisions for them. It did provide data to be used for good decision-making.

More than a decade has passed since my discovery. The astounding practical results of the system over the years have demonstrated that God gives everyone a unique set of vocational gifts. SIMA helps people understand what work they are thereby gifted to do. And it has helped me realize that work is not merely the means by which we put bread on the table. Work is also the place where we can be fulfilled. People tie their identities to the work they do. "I am a carpenter" and "I am a doctor" are much more likely to be heard than "I do carpentering" or "I do doctoring."

There are those who would argue against making the subject of work so important. Among them are those who did not have golden opportunities and whose work has little or no relationship to who they are. Others believe the search for fulfillment in work is senseless because true fulfillment is found only through devotion to and communion with God.

I trust the remainder of this book will provide an adequate response to both positions. At this introductory point, however, I would simply point out that most people do expect more from work than just the capacity to pay their heating bills.

The desire to find fulfillment in one's work has been made clear to me through individuals I have known who have varied greatly in their hopes, goals, and accomplishments. One has pursued wealth and attained it; another sought fame and got wealth with it; and another has striven for both and not even come close to either. Still another believes both objectives to be worthless. Here is a student trying to select one goal out of all the possibilities he sees, and another hasn't but a vague idea of what he should pursue. All, however diverse the situations, share the common concern about who they are or will be in their work.

Perhaps they have a sense of calling. Perhaps we all do, and in spite of the mistakes we make and the dead ends we take, we are attempting to fulfill that calling and become the people we were designed to be.

If that is true, it is crucial not only to discover what our calling is, regardless of our present station in life, but also to bring it about. I trust that the remainder of this book will be useful to the reader in accomplishing both those goals. But I need to issue a warning. If you like the abstract, you may prefer part 2 of the book because it is directed to how we *think* about work. If you are a practical person, you may prefer part 3, where the focus is on applications. Remember, whether you are one or the other, what we think is intimately related to what we do. We need to pay attention to both.

Ralph Mattson
1982

PART I
FAITH AT WORK?

1

The Great Divide—
Sunday and Monday

CONFUSION ABOUT ONE'S PLACE IN THE WORLD
can start quite early, as it did for us, being brought up in New
York City and Chicago. We did not realize our confusion,
because we were gradually initiated into it and did not have a
perspective with which to judge.

Some things were clear, such as the appearance of good
and evil. Good was Mr. Murphy making sure each day that
seventy-five-year-old Mrs. Carlson in the apartment above was
all right, even though she never expressed any gratitude. Good
was the free kosher pickle from the owner of the delicatessen or
the stories Mr. Koster told about his youth in Europe.

Evil was seeing a household of furniture out on the street with
an evicted, distraught woman wailing for help. Or it was Mr.
Johnson drunkenly swearing from the street at his family, who
had locked him out for the hundredth time. Evil was also the
constantly innovative ways people had of cheating in the stores
and street markets.

In contrast to the environment and philosophy of the city were
the teachings of the church. There another attitude reigned, and
different values were taught. Christian men and women spoke
of God and His purposes. Sometimes they spoke sanctimoni-
ously, and sometimes unrealistically, but whatever flaws we
discovered, whatever failures we perceived, this minority of
people expressed an authority that belied their numbers. They
were able to counter the bad influences of the streets with a
convincing proclamation of the gospel.

We were also aware of a strict separation between the church and the world surrounding it. Our lives were divided between the life of school, work, and the streets and the life of home and the church. We learned to slip easily from one world into the other and back again.

Full-time Service

Given what they experienced daily in the city, it is no surprise that the Christians of our youth saw little of value outside the church doors. Their lives were divided into the life of work in the world for physical survival and life in the church for spiritual growth. Though Christian parents were proud when one of their children found success in the world, their greatest hope was that one of their children would enter "full-time service." For a Roman Catholic family, that meant a son's becoming a priest or a daughter's entering a convent. For us Protestants, it meant going to Bible school or seminary (depending on one's denomination) and becoming a preacher, missionary, or evangelist. This was, *and often still is*, believed to be the ultimate achievement of faith. From this acme of full-time service, all other part-time evangelizing, acts of charity, ministry, and community involvement arranged themselves in a descending order of spirituality. It was as if a class structure existed in the Christian community, with the "full-time servant of God" towering above the rest.

Unfortunately, it is still common for Christians to feel that increased church activity equals heightened spirituality. They assume that the sum of Christianity is telling others about Jesus Christ and being active in church, charity, and piety. Most Christians do agree that those things are an embodiment of the teachings and commands of our Lord. But we question, Do they represent the whole of what God intends for His children? Do they totally reveal God's plan for our lives?

What about the Other 80 Percent of My Life?

Does this view of what it means to be a Christian make sense when we face the reality of our jobs, where we spend most of our time? Too often our jobs are seen only as a place to witness about God and perform good works. Even when a vocation involves a quasi-religious activity, such as teaching, counseling, doctoring, or servicing people's material needs, it is hard for many Christians to see how their jobs could advance God's causes. After all, these jobs involve technologies that have their origins in worldly systems, so Christians must function as their non-Christian associates do.

Home activities are also rarely seen as spiritual in nature. Cleaning, cooking, sleeping, watching television, reading books, redecorating, reorganizing, renovating, playing games, enjoying one another, dealing with one another, serving one another—all are part of living, but what have they to do with Christian living? Yes, one might have some Bible study and prayer, but it is hard to keep faithful to it, and the kids yawn and squirm. Is this domestic scene one of a family living out faith? What is wrong? It seems for the most part that one does what the neighbors do.

Sacred and Secular

When facing doubts about whether God's will could ever relate to daily life, you might seek out a spiritual advisor and express guilt about the duality of life. Many counselors will try to reassure you by pointing out that your work is as important to God as their own ministry. But they may not show you where or how or why. So even though you leave feeling better, a week later the doubts return.

You might react by throwing yourself anew into one or another Christian activity, spending most of your evenings and weekends doing so. One day, perhaps after your spouse complains about feeling deserted, or after being assigned some particularly interesting project at work, you begin to wonder again about the relevance of God and His will to your life. Or more accurately, you begin to question seriously whether your vocation or your family role was or ever would be an expression of God's will for your life. More than one husband and father or wife and mother, new to the faith, has expressed a longing for

the day when he or she would be free from work and domestic
chores to "really follow the Lord."

You may look to the pastor and his ministry as a vicarious
involvement in "spiritual" matters, together, of course, with
your own occasional, direct stints at ushering or serving as an
elder or deacon. Tragically, if this process continues, the apparent irrelevance of faith to everyday life, the seeming hopelessness of finding an answer short of full-time Christian service,
might cool your first love, and harden your heart to new spiritual
experience thereby halting maturation.

But strangely enough, even if you exchanged your life for one
"more spiritual," you would face again the things you had
hoped to desert. The missionary, the evangelist, the parish priest
and minister, the spiritual counselor, and the community
leader—all spend most of their time doing things that unmistak-
ably resemble the maintenance, administrative, troubleshoot-
ing, detail-doing, getting ready, and cleaning up tasks performed by their secular brothers and sisters. Of course, there is
the redeeming conviction that these deeds are being done for the
church. But even that assumption is questionable, as we will see
later.

Seeking Meaning

While many Christians have given up trying to apply their
faith to everyday life, others still search for the fulfillment
promised in conversion and assured throughout Scripture. They
want their earthly years to overflow with meaning. Are we
converted merely to see others converted, who in turn are to see
to it that others are converted, each in turn embracing evangelism as his sole reason for being? Surely God wants more
from us and for us.

Evangelism is important, and the Bible teaches that it is a
major responsibility of the church and, consequently, of each
believer. All Christians are soldiers in a massive spiritual battle
for the souls of men. But evangelism, as an end in and of itself,

is patently absurd. Those who base their lives on such an idea
dilute their own effectiveness as soul-winners by attracting
people susceptible to salesmanship rather than by winning
people to a Christ-centered lifestyle, a way of living that radically alters their direction and purpose. Evangelism brings us *to*
the Kingdom, but once we have entered, we must seek the
purpose of being *in* the Kingdom.

Because of this thirst for meaning, many Christians seek
enrichment of their worship and living and are drawn to specialized Christian groups that promise deeper spiritual experiences.
The passion for Christ and Christian living can be replaced by a
preoccupation with a particular doctrinal emphasis, or a special
lifestyle, or a way of operating. The potential for full-orbed
Christian living may wither.

The specialized groups, however, may offer a more intimate
fellowship and may at least attempt to grapple with the practical
side of faith.

The Church's Concern with Itself

Failing to distinguish between life as an institution and life in
the world through its members, churches are too often concerned with their institutional roles. When that happens, they
end up working primarily for their own survival and growth.

That in turn forces Christians to assume that only what is
done at or for the church provides an adequate religious life.
The thinking goes, *If I worship at my church on Sunday, if I
tithe, if I reach out to a brother in need, if I evangelize, if I avoid
sin, if I spend a fair amount of time in the Bible, if I help when
I'm asked—I am then leading a spiritual life and as near as I can
determine, I am fulfilling God's entire purpose for my life.*

Obviously, any Christian who adequately covers those responsibilities has done well. But limiting one's spiritual activities to those traditionally associated with the church isolates
faith as if Jesus Christ is irrelevant to the worlds of art, music,
literature, mining, farming, banking and finance, politics,

manufacturing, commerce, insurance, fishing, food service, and on and on—one of which is the average believer's world most of the time!

Does God Care?

Is God concerned about how good a farmer, homemaker, secretary, or salesman we are? Is God concerned about the quality of our leisure activities? Is God concerned about all the things we do that we would label secular?

Many Christians would answer yes but mean merely that God is interested in those areas to the degree that they become places to display piety—the fact that we are good, patient, kind, and selective in what we do.

Those saints of our childhood would enthusiastically agree. They also demonstrated what they believed as they adroitly maintained their integrity while dealing with the often-difficult realities of their workworld. Their joy emerged from the knowledge of pleasing God with the quality of their character as they negotiated their way among people who expected them to cheat, lie, and cut corners like everybody else.

A demonstration of honesty, faithfulness, and discipline was serious business for God's people, and they trusted rightfully that God would reward them for it. Quality of character was the issue. God would judge their work according to the character it produced in them. Though we believe a great deal more can be said about work, nothing more important than that will be said.

It is not our intention to diminish the importance of showing the reality of God's power in our lives by doing good works. But we insist that it is not enough. If it were, what kind of work we do would not make any difference if we did it well. But we believe that what in particular you do makes a profound difference.

Other religions can demonstrate piety in good works. What is unique about biblical religion is that it addresses the God who works by the power of the Holy Spirit, the same Spirit who brought into being the entire creation and the potential for what we call civilization. The Spirit who called us into life also calls us into *purpose* in life.

What Does God Want?

Many Christians want to simplify things by telling us that all we need to do is individually find God's will for our lives and pursue it, whatever it turns out to be.

That's a familiar theme to us. Early in our lives, teaching and preaching repeatedly urged us to place the satisfaction of God's will as our foremost concern. That made some sense to us; even as children we could understand that we could give pleasure to God through obedient behavior, much the same as our obedience gave our parents pleasure.

Who can argue against such an idea? However, the problem arises when we become practical. Most of us do not have visions such as the apostle Paul had. We do not clearly hear the voice of God directing us. Though there is evidence of God's calling and directing individuals through the centuries, most of us have great difficulty in discovering God's will for our careers and future.

One brother confronting the difficulty could have been speaking for thousands of Christians:

Look, I know I should be following God's will. Though I'm imperfect, I am seriously committed to Christ and do not need to be convinced whether or not I should find His will. I am most eager to find it beyond the dos and don'ts of my everyday life. It would solve a considerable number of problems if I could. The difficulty resides in the elusiveness of God's plan for my life. To be honest, I wonder at the game being played, where we are urged to seek and follow what seems to be completely hidden. Why do we need to convince God that we want our Christian lives to be relevant? Why can't He give us the blueprint for us to carry out? What career should I pursue? What am I supposed to be doing with my life? What is His will?

PART II
GOD GIVEN

2

Understanding God's Will

"WHAT IS GOD'S WILL FOR MY LIFE?" IS A question that is usually asked in hopes that the answer will identify a specific vocation. Since work and vocations are the theme of this book, we will address them in subsequent chapters. But we will be far richer in our working and our living if we understand the *why* as well as the *what* of what we should do with our lives.

If we are to understand this, we need to perceive more of God's personality and character. Let us focus on God's will as an expression of Himself.

God's Will as an Expression of Himself

Obviously, prior to creation when all there was, was God, God's will was not directed to anyone but Himself. In the society of His own Trinity, He willed His own good. It had nothing to do with a choice between good and evil. There was no evil, there was no need to choose. If we could have come into contact with His will then, it would have been to touch the center of God's personality, the ultimate wonder of life Himself.

In making this point, we open up a number of theological questions that cannot be dealt with here. But at least we can see that God's will has more to do with God's being and life and less to do with making decisions. It is only when God's will appears in the history of man that it brings the necessity of choice between life and death, good and evil.

At the stroke of creation, when it became possible to conceive of someone other than God, it then became possible to choose between the two. And from that point until now, the question of God's will is one that necessitates choosing. Now obedience becomes possible.

God honors obedience whether it's plodding and faithful or joyful. The latter, however, increases the quality of our Christian living and also more favorably impresses those who observe it. So we intend on these pages to encourage joyful obedience.

In contrast to the view that God's will is an expression of Himself, let us look at two other characterizations of God and His nature that frequently make their appearance. One we will call "the moody God," the other "the dictator God."

Both of them come from a common mistake mankind has repeatedly made, namely, to read into God's nature the distortions of our own nature. Worshiping such a self-made god is a form of idolatry, and we are all guilty of it to some degree.

The moody God

In the first false view, God's will is seen as an expression of divine but transient moods, especially in reaction to human endeavors, good or evil—but especially evil. People who see God in this way expect His wrath at the least mistake and assume when things go wrong that it is a sure sign of God's condemnation. They tend to forget that the Christian does not have some magical protection against the difficulties all men face. Jesus Christ Himself did not have it easy, so why should we expect to be exempted?

As Christians, troubles are often due simply to our being pilgrims in an alien land. We need not blame an unpredictable God for these. Such unpredictability does not square with Scripture. The God of the Bible is not moody and is certainly not fickle. The apostle James described God as one "with whom there is no variation or shadow due to change" (James 1:17 RSV). In the Old Testament we also have the simple statement, "For I the LORD do not change" (Mal. 3:6 RSV).

The truth is that God is consistent and dependable. His consistency is an essential part of His nature and justifies not only mere trust, but even unconditional trust. In Him we can find ultimate security.

The dictator God

The other distorted picture of God's will arises from the view that we are slaves and God is a master, who on occasion we might describe (if we dared) as tyrannical. God's will reflects a divine determination to have everything His way. We feel required to yield since ultimately He is going to win anyway. He is stronger. There is certainly truth in the idea that God always ultimately wins, but since He intends our ultimate good, we can be considerably cheered by knowing that He must win. But if we see our role in terms of mere fatalistic obedience, we distort the picture that Scripture gives us. In the Bible, we see God engaging us as partners and giving us power to act aggressively as co-workers by providing a means for us to change circumstances through prayer, repentance, and the exercise of our gifts. Here are several examples of such Scriptures:

First of all, then, I urge that supplications, prayers, intercessions, and thanksgivings be made for all men (1 Tim. 2:1 RSV).

The prayer of a righteous man has great power in its effects (James 5:16 RSV).

If my people . . . humble themselves, and pray and seek my face, and turn from their wicked ways, . . . I . . . will forgive their sin and heal their land (2 Chron. 7:14 RSV).

It is clear that our will as expressed in prayer does have effect. Many biblical events show that God's will and man's will have a strong mutual impact on situations. The cooperation of divine and human wills is an exciting compound and certainly does not suggest we are lackeys merely carrying out the wishes of the eternal boss. God's will already has our good imbedded in it, and obedience to such a will is to cooperate with an enormous power determined to bless us. God invites our involvement. The blessings do not come by fate, but by faith.

God's Will Is Joy

Now that we have a couple of examples of what God's will is not, let us look at what it is and say more about the joy, life, and wonder that obedience brings.

A most helpful view of God's will comes through an understanding of the gospel stories about Jesus Christ. In all the roles Christ fulfilled on earth, whether as healer, teacher, redeemer, or friend, we can identify Him as the ultimate demonstration of God's will. Jesus was at once the product of and the enactor of—but above all, the fulfiller of—divine will. He said, "For I came down from heaven, not to do mine own will, but the will of him that sent me" (John 6:38 KJV). The script of Jesus' life, called "The Father's Will," had been written before His birth, and it included a horrible death.

Why did Christ embrace the Father's will so fully even though it meant extraordinary emotional and spiritual pain as well as physical torture? What was worth this price? The answer is in the striking words of Hebrews 12:2: "Jesus . . . who for the joy that was set before him endured the cross" (KJV).

Jesus did it (at least in part) for joy.

It is only when we see the denouement of the story that the plot makes any sense. If we isolate the occurrences at Calvary from the enthroned Christ at the right hand of the Father, all we are left with is an empty tragedy. If we take the view that Christ had and keep our eyes on the ultimate target, however, we are encouraged to do God's will because it will lead to joy. Like Jesus, we will discover the reality of bliss that is at the end of any path the Father may send us down, difficult or otherwise.

God's Will Is Pleasure

Many Christians are confused about the subject of pleasure. They are suspicious even though the old catechism states that the chief end of man is to know God and *enjoy* Him forever.

We can understand the Christian's suspicion, however, for Satan has captured thousands by exploiting pleasure, and we must be cautious lest we, too, be deluded. But we also need to realize that the reason so many can be captured by pleasure is that we human beings are made for pleasure. Remember the phrase from the Psalms, "At thy right hand there are pleasures for evermore" (Psalm 16:11 KJV).

Apparently we cannot be in God's presence without experiencing pleasure. It is a natural result of being with Him. Not only has He built into us a deep capacity for experiencing pleasure now, but He also expands that capacity so we can enjoy Him forevermore. As we live on earth, pleasure is frequently interrupted by pain. However, that is not to be a permanent condition. When we are going through times of pain, it is good to know that in eternity there is no pain.

C. S. Lewis in *The Screwtape Letters* reminded us that God alone is the author of pleasure, and though Satan exploits it for his own devious ends, he cannot create one pleasure. In fact, his only interest in pleasure is as bait, for once the capture takes place, his intention is to remove quickly the satisfaction of pleasure and replace it with unfulfilled desire.

Hell is clearly not the place of pleasure and satisfaction, but heaven is. God has no quarrel with pleasure itself. Satan does. God's wrath is directed toward shapeless pleasure, toward pleasure snatched by ignoring His rules, toward pleasure that eventually cannot be pleasure.

The rules of God (the will of God) are not intended to prevent pleasure, but to protect our capacity for pleasure. To pursue pleasure on our terms instead of His is to court disaster. It will cut us off from the eventual ecstatic realization of God, whom to know will be ultimate pleasure. By this, we do not mean merely "Know God so you can know pleasure." What we mean is "Know God, but realize you cannot do so without pleasure."

A discussion of pleasure is also a good place to consider another interesting image of God's will. Jesus said in John 4:34, "My meat is to do the will of him that sent me" (KJV). That means more than necessity. The Father's will was Jesus' ultimate source of life. It was His sustenance, possessing color and texture and taste as of good food. It was as substantial as roasted fish, as tasty as a loaf of bread, as satisfying as a cup of water. It nourished and strengthened Him and delighted His eyes.

The idea we propose is no exaggeration. Review the nature and place of Jesus' first miracle, His symbolizing Himself as bread and, at another time, as a permanently satisfying drink. Consider the final elevation of bread and wine as emblems of His life and history; anticipate the wedding supper of the Lamb. We can see in all these a remarkable transformation of the common experience of eating.

There is a little incident in Jesus' life that we can use to enhance all this. In John 21, we read about one of Christ's appearances after the Resurrection. Jesus' companions were out fishing, having left the night before. When Christ appeared on the shore, He saw His friends at their prebreakfast toil. Jesus shouted some advice about successful fishing, and, anticipating they would soon be headed in, He quickly prepared to roast some fish. In your imagination, can you see Him gathering sticks for a fire and saving several good ones to skewer the fish? Can you see His expression as He calculates how long it will take to have the fish broiled to their succulent best when the boat touches shore? Can you sense His anticipation of the fishermen's pleasure as they, having begun the day rowing and hauling fishnets, realize that breakfast is ready? Can you see them gathered around the fire, enthusiastically sharing large morsels of juicy, tender fish and the delight of Jesus for pulling it off so well?

This is the One who talked about the will of His Father as the food that sustained Him. Not an abstract image, it came out of everyday experience and so can appeal to us all.

At least three times a day, every day, we have reminders of what God's will is like.

David, a poet-ancestor of Jesus, also conceived of God's will in terms of food. He wrote that it was "sweeter also than honey and drippings of the honeycomb" (Psalm 20:10 RSV).

Why the enthusiasm?

In Old Testament times, the primary expression of God's will was the law as given to Moses. The law gave shape to society and family relations, to government and morality. It defined good and evil. David understood the magnitude of this foundational blessing and how it imparted meaning to his culture and life, so he sang its description as golden, free-flowing, sweet-tasting honey. How much more should Christians delight in the will of God as now revealed in Jesus Christ, a much sweeter revelation? We can gladly participate in Christ's response to the Father's will and delight ourselves in its manifestation, especially since it scoops us up in its intention to bring us into the source of all pleasure.

God's Will Is Beauty

Somewhere as a child you may have read a story about a cantankerous character attempting, unsuccessfully, to get the hero to do something. All argument remains unpersuasive until a beautiful young damsel (usually the grump's daughter) intercedes, smiles demurely, and makes the same request, but with spectacular results. Beauty conquers, and the hero is off to his task!

Why does the Christian seek to know God's will for his life? Because he is compelled to? Nothing else makes sense? It is dangerous not to? All three are good reasons, and we should note their validity. However, singing above these is the winsome voice of ultimate and astounding beauty. We can be wooed into action by a King whose servants willingly lay down their lives for the sake of gazing eternally into *His* face, hearing the voice of *His* approval. It is almost an erotic compulsion like that expressed in the Song of Solomon: "The voice of my beloved! Behold, he comes, leaping upon the mountains, bounding over the hills" (2:8 RSV). If you want to last the battle, if you want to make it to the end, be possessed by, fall in love with, be captivated by the beauty of the ultimate King.

To write of God's beauty is obviously not to say everything about God, but it does direct us to the source of a most potent, motivating force. Though the fear of God's judgment is an undeniable fact of our existence, we are psychologically unable to maintain a sustained emotional response to it. God's beauty, however much it may vary in expression, is a correct, continual dwelling place for our hearts and wills.

Finally, consider the universe that is a product of God's will.

Is it a surprise that it is beautiful to our eyes and minds? If there is any attractiveness in the form of trees, the shape of mountains, the sound of brooks; if there is a sense of delight in stars, skies, and weather, then we have evidence of God's beauty.

No work of art can be greater than its creator. A product must always be less than its source. The origin of a melody is a person, and he is always greater than the song. This forces us to conclude after contemplating the beauty of creation that the Creator of such must be more beautiful. He must be incomprehensively wonderful to behold.

The beauty of God transcends the silence between the leaves; the dance of the galaxies; the grandeur of deserts, mountains, and oceans; the polish of an autumn apple; and all He has made. Creation, even in its fallen state, convinces us of the reality of divine beauty. It assures us that the result of our willingness to abandon ourselves to His intentions can only be further beauty. God makes no ungraceful moves, and as we are individually embraced by His will, we find that our lives are richer, our former emptiness now full of grace.

3

Responding to God's Will

WHAT WE THINK OF GOD'S WILL MAKES A DIF-
ference. What we do in response to it is also important. God's
will, by nature, is that which requires response.

In the heavenly realm, the response to God's will is essentially harmonious and a result of a clear vision of God. In our
case, because of the Fall, even when we intend to do God's will,
we not only have a problem in understanding what it is, but we
also have difficulty carrying it out. We are not left to make our
own way, however. The Holy Spirit works within us to bring
about increasing understanding that is applied to the decision-
making process of each Christian. Its expression varies from
person to person. But there are some general comments to be
made about how we should respond to God that are true for all
Christians.

Loving Response

We must respond to God's will with love. If we consider love
only in terms of emotion, we are going to have great difficulty,
since most of us can only maintain our emotional reaction to
God for short periods of time, and then perhaps only when
circumstances happen to arouse and support those feelings. We
may go through a specially meaningful prayer time or an uplifting worship service, or we may have responded to a particularly
beautiful expression of God's creation. Any one of those experiences can stir up a genuine emotional appreciation of God's
involvement with us or just the wonder of who He is in Himself.
Those are good times and should be cherished, but they are

transient and stand in contrast against most of our living experiences.

In teaching how to respond to the Father, Jesus referred to the Scripture, "You must love the Lord your God with all your heart and soul and strength." He was using Deuteronomy 6 as His source. In studying that chapter, we discover that we are not only called to love, but to serve and obey as well. That indicates the balance to be sought in loving God. On the one hand, we are dealing with feelings, emotions, spirit, enthusiasm, and affection. On the other hand, we need obedience, working, serving, and behaving. The first has to do with our passion for God, the second with our actions before God.

With All Your Heart

When Jesus spoke of love, He spoke of intense feelings and in terms of power. There is no getting around the energetic words that embellish the Scriptures: *glory, life, abundant life, wonder,* and *joy* are but a few that are common.

There is also no escaping the contrast to the realities of day-to-day living, where the words *monotonous, lifeless, boring,* and *mediocre* are often justified. These latter qualities can be expected in the lives of nonbelievers who are estranged from the source of life and so find life dull. We can understand their pursuit of greener pastures, better jobs, more success, more money, and more escape, since each attainment fails to satisfy for very long. It is no surprise that artificial stimulus or escape becomes commonplace for them. Entertainment becomes a paramount interest, and the pursuit of "fun" a necessity.

However, if we find Christians looking for the same pleasures—but of course, in the context of Christian culture—observers might wonder if the church has embraced an empty illusion in the gospel. A church caught in the spirit of Madison Avenue and show business can scarcely be considered a dynamic expression of God's will. It is preoccupied with appearances and fails to recognize that the glory of the Christian comes from within.

As Christians, we must reject the world's version of life and the imitations that appear in the church. Though we are members of an eternal kingdom, we do not look for external appearances of that Kingdom's splendor. It is hidden within us.

Children of the King

In spite of appearances, we are royalty; we are children of the heavenly King. Remaining as we do in this world, temporarily separated from the Kingdom that is our home, our neighbors see no royal robes or display of our wealth. We are nevertheless princes and princesses of the Kingdom.

It is the Spirit himself bearing witness with our spirit that we are children of God, and if children, then heirs, heirs of God and fellow heirs with Christ, provided we suffer with him in order that we may also be glorified with him (Rom. 8:16, 17 RSV).

An unrevealed splendor has embraced us. It is reality. It was reality when the above Scripture was written, and it is reality now.

We may seem unimportant and unknown in the world. We may seem inconsequential from almost anybody's point of view. Because of this, it may be difficult for us to see where the splendor is, especially if we are going through troubled circumstances. Since we know ourselves to be children of God, we cannot agree with how others see us. Sight may say we are of little worth, one among millions. Spiritual insight will say otherwise. Faith says we are God's heirs with Jesus Christ. We have been named and called by God.

So we do not lose heart. Though our outer nature is wasting away, our inner nature is being renewed every day. For this slight momentary affliction is preparing for us an eternal weight of glory beyond all comparison, because we look not to the things that are seen but to the things that are unseen; for the things that are seen are transient, but the things that are unseen are eternal (2 Cor. 4:16–18 RSV).

With our eyes fixed on the unseen, we can view what is seen in our everyday life with a different attitude. In the ardor of our

love for God, we can believe that He transforms the meaning of
our daily actions.

When that happens, we can become excited about God.
Instead of reacting to Him with religious devotion, we may
discover a capacity for God-centered passion.

God only is reality. Passionate response to God is possible
only when we live in the awareness of reality, aware of what is
actually happening, not preoccupied by the illusions of appearance. The Christian should interpret the appearances of things
according to reality, not vice-versa. We are to have a renewed
vision. Our sight should be formed by the realities of faith so
that we see things working together according to the purposes of
God for ultimate good; so that things, objects, and people are
seen in the context of the drama God is bringing about. Otherwise, even the beauty of the world will have a transient effect.

God's Enthusiasm about You

In our first encounter with God at conversion, we may have
been confused in our concern with our sin and hopelessness, so
we did not perceive anything more than the idea that God moved
toward us and loved us. When we began to grow as Christians,
we realized that God had more than a casual interest in us. He
wasn't just helping us along. He was on our side, and He was
enthusiastic about us.

Look at this wonderful gem of a Scripture from Jeremiah
20:11a: "The LORD is on my side, strong and ruthless" (NEB).

The singlemindedness of that word *ruthless* is stunning.
Godly passion stretches over the centuries from then to now
God has spoken, He has acted, and He is enticing us into His
Kingdom. Why He should do so is beyond our knowing. All we
can say is that it has something to do with His unpredictable (but
not inconsistent) character. He has no need for us, but He wants
us.

He certainly does not require our company, so we dare not be
coy. This is not the plot of some delicate love affair. This is the
God who has smashed the wall of partition between Himself

and us, who has spent blood and somehow entered spaces of horror to bring about reconciliation with us at a gruesome price. There is no further extension possible. He has moved ultimately, and no additional steps can be taken.

This God can shake us out of the lethargy of ordinary living and loving to be awakened to exciting possibilities— possibilities that lay at hand, not the impossible goals of daydreams.

But there is more. It is indeed a wonder to discover that the Creator of the universe, the Author of all things, the Ultimate One loves you and has manipulated your history so that you may know that truth. But when you look up and discover that the One who loves you is extraordinarily beautiful, infinitely handsome, your situation is nothing less than astounding. The ordinary day becomes extraordinary, because it is one in a chain of days that will lead you into the place where you can not only gaze insatiably upon that beauty, but also be joined into and become one with it.

If you want a scriptural portrayal of the scenario, immerse yourself in the poetry of the Song of Solomon. It is a fine display of passion, and it supports in the spirit of its verse the essence of what we are saying here. All the stodgy interpretations ever applied to that book cannot dull the clear, exquisite picture of one passionate lover longing for another.

While it is primarily a romantic poem of love, it is also seen as a display of how God feels about the church, exemplified by all the individuals in it. We can conclude that if God actually loves us with such passion, it is a wonder that cannot leave us untouched.

Acting Out Your Love for God

Passionate love, whether maternal or erotic, usually leads to some kind of expression. Love that is never demonstrated is incomplete love. An obvious example of completed love is erotic love, which is expressed in the act of sex. But in all loves, there is the desire to do something for someone. "I wish I could

do something for her." "I want to do something for him."
Friends want to "do something together." Those are familiar
phrases to us because they are basic to caring affection and
concern.

In our relationships with other people, only certain acts are
selected as expressing love. Often they are acts determined by
the needs of the loved one (or at least they are acts to which the
loved one will respond). In loving God, however, there are no
acts that we can direct to His needs, because by nature God has
no needs. The acts we can direct to Him are based on another
kind of relationship, that of the created to the Creator.

We please God when we act the way we are designed to act,
when we are who God designed us to be. When such actions are
carried out with the intention of being expressions of love to
Him, they do in fact become expressions of love to Him.

A Metaphor in Art

God's delight in His creation of man may be likened to that of
a sculptor in his sculpture. As the work comes progressively
closer to the artist's intention, the more it delights the maker and
becomes more vital. In your imagination, impart free will to the
sculpture and see how wonderful the willing cooperation of the
sculpture to the intention of the artist becomes. Conversely,
perceive how hideous it would be for the sculpture to refuse to
become what the artist is designing, particularly when it has no
capacity in itself to design or form itself. Its only possibility for
being is in the hands of the sculptor. Not to cooperate with the
artist's intentions is to deny its existence as art. It is to deny
itself.

The complementary relationship between God and man,
sculptor and sculpture, can be illustrated further in the relationship of husband and wife. In sexuality, the masculine is discovered in feminity, the feminine in masculinity. Man and woman
discover their respective natures, not in themselves, but in each
other. So we discover our createdness, our being, in the Creator, and so He knows Himself as Creator in us.

However, a difference must remain. Because we are created, we can only discover our full nature in Him. He, on the other hand, being the uncreated, self-sufficient One, does not need us in order to discover His full nature. He knows Himself fully in the eternal, self-reflective society of the Trinity.

Honoring God in Ordinary Acts

Realizing that actions can be expressions of love to God, since they express our created natures, allows us to realize also that except for sinful activities, *all acts are potentially useful in demonstrating our love for God.*

Most activities are quite ordinary and are common to people all over the world, especially the necessary things we do for survival, such as eating and drinking. Scripture teaches that for the Christian, ordinary acts are in reality quite special. They can be accomplished in such a way, with such an attitude, that they actually honor God. The apostle Paul taught us this in 1 Corinthians 10:31 when he stated, "Whether you eat or drink, or whatever you do, do all to the glory of God" (RSV).

In that verse, the mundane is swallowed up by the sublime. The ordinary becomes the ground for worship. A man can sit at his table and celebrate with his family, using dishes and utensils, aware of who created things, enjoying the taste and sustenance of food, knowing the inventor of taste and existence. He can do the same with odd jobs around the house or in playing.

The modern mind has been so secular in its day-to-day thinking that even those who are relatively sensitive to spiritual things fail to grasp the testimony to God that is all about us. As a result, portions of the Old Testament seem to be archaic curiosities and fail to open our eyes to glory. Consider the following verse as an example: "For you shall go out in joy, and be led forth in peace; the mountains and the hills before you shall break forth into singing, and all the trees of the field shall clap their hands" (Isa. 55:12 RSV). Singing mountains and clapping trees are poetic expressions, certainly, but poetic expressions of what? Nothing less than creation praising

Creator? How? By each element of creation—animal, vegetable, mineral—being what it was made to be.

We honor God when we demonstrate our creatureliness, doing that which we as human beings are equipped by Him to do. It may be expressed in the usual. It may be demonstrated in something extraordinary. Which it is does not matter to God at all. What does matter is that we are being who we are designed to be as descendants of Adam.

If the lower orders of creation praise God in their own natures, how much more should man, the highest level of creation, do?

Because man is a fallen creature, he has not only been cut off from seeing the continuum of praise issuing forth from the entire universe, but he has also lost the lead position in that mighty chorus.

Jesus Himself knew Psalm 104 in His triumphal entry into Jerusalem, when we see man and creation coming closest to having the Lord as earthly King. He silenced the Pharisees' complaints with the claim that if man did not praise, the very stones would cry out in praise (see Luke 19:40). He also might have been thinking about these verses from Psalm 148:

"Praise Him, sun and moon,
    praise Him, all you shining stars!
Praise Him, you highest heavens,
    and you waters above the heavens! . . .

Mountains and all hills,
    fruit trees and all cedars!
Beasts and all cattle,
    creeping things and flying birds!

Kings of the earth and all peoples,
    princes and all rulers of the earth!
Young men and maidens together,
    old men and children!

Let them praise the name of the LORD" (vv. 3, 4, 9–13 RSV).

Man praises God not only in ritual, but also in his work. In the previously mentioned Psalm 104, we discover a picture of a God who clothes and houses Himself with nature. Nature includes the winds and clouds in their places, the plants and animals in their places, and man in his place. In verse 23, man is pictured taking his place in creation by going to work!

Divine Ecology

When man takes his correct position in creation, divine ecology falls into place and praise naturally emerges. Competence then manifests itself in work and play. It can take place at a ticket or sales counter, in a restaurant, or in the Post Office. Even if the performer is not a Christian, if he is doing what he is gifted to do, he demonstrates how it ought to be done (see Psalm 68:18, 19).

The incompetency we see everywhere is not because people lack gifts, but because they are not in the right place for their gifts. They are not being stewards of what God has given them. There are plenty of gifts to do all the work that needs to be done everywhere and to do all of it gloriously well—so well, in fact, that people would go rejoicing from day to day over how much was accomplished and how well it was accomplished. But the world's systems, corrupted by the sin of man, place enormous obstacles in the way of each person who attempts to find his rightful place in creation. Such systems assume that people and creation are mere fodder for their intentions.

In short, most Christians as well as non-Christians do not understand what a job means and cannot address the world on the matter of the widespread waste of human resources. Therefore, they cannot make a redemptive difference. They are cut off from the whole vision of worship through work. They view such scriptures as "the trees of the wild shall clap their hands" as Jewish poetic peculiarities that have no relation to the fluorescent-lighted offices of large corporations and the daily details of any job.

The result is too many Christians performing incompetent, second-rate work, replacing the biblical command to redeem the time with an intention to "put in some time," an unsatisfactory result for the world and for the Kingdom.

What would be the impact of a church whose individual members knew their rightful place of work in a world where the majority of workers are misfits? With what kind of authority does the Christian speak when he knows his place in the scheme of the universe? How would Christian education be viewed if it actually provided young people with an understanding of their specific gifts and equipped them accordingly?

4

Work: God's Idea

IT MUST HAVE BEEN ASTONISHING FOR THE Greek of Old Testament times, who relegated physical work to slaves and other inferiors, to discover that the God of the Jews actually worked. How curious to have a story of Jehovah who worked over creation for six days and rested for only one day (see Gen. 2:2). What a curious allotment of time to be ascribed to divinity!

The fact that God worked is a good place for us, who are made in His image, to discover what work actually means. Why would God work?

There are those who would answer that God had to work in order to create, and He had to create in order to overcome His loneliness. Those Christians, who ought to know better, write about creation as if it were a necessity for God to create, as if it gave Him a purpose. They go on to propose that God is love, and that love needs an object, so God created man to be the object of His love.

What an appalling idea—a lonely God!

A lonely God is an incomplete god, a needy god, a god dependent upon our existence and, therefore, imperfect and not God at all. For anyone to worship such a god is to worship a creation of man's pride. Consider the infinity of God and try to reconcile that reality with the flash we call time. Whatever did God do "prior" to the creation of time and man's arrival if He needed us? If we also understand that the "prior time" is eternal, the whole idea is seen to be absurd.

43

God's Self-sufficiency

The God of the Bible is eternally self-sufficient. He enjoys the society of His own Trinity and has no need of another. We have the need of others since we are dependent by nature and cannot exist on our own. We begin life helpless, requiring parents to provide for us. As adults, we need others' skills to provide what we cannot. Psychologically, we need others for socialization, without which we cannot fully discover our self-identity.

In our relationship to God, we need Him, but He does not need us. Our love for Him is the way to survival, but His love for us is freely given. He receives no benefit from our love. Even our gratitude and praise add nothing to God. His encouragement of worship is for our sake, that we gain a right perspective by turning away from our limited view to consider the source of all life, blessing, and power. When we have celebrated God and worshiped, we turn back to our labors and problems with renewed spirits and realistic perspective. To worship is to see the way things really are. It is never to add to God, since that is absolutely impossible. God is all in all and not a total to which anything can be added. He is complete in Himself.

God did not work at creating the universe to fulfill a need within Himself. The word *need* or any other word suggesting a lack attached to God is ludicrous.

What shall we do, then, with God's work? How can we explain creation if it was not required by God? The act of creation and the reality of God's self-sufficiency are irreconcilable, so we must accept a paradox. We can say something (though not a complete answer) that does make sense to our spiritual intuition.

We believe creation is due to the exuberance of God. His work is a divine gesture reflective of a bountiful nature. It has no purpose in terms of fulfilling a need in God, but is a pleasure to Him. The fact that creation is for God's pleasure does not diminish its worth. Creation is ripe with meaning, since God

Himself has breathed into our beings the vitality of His own life. The corridors of time are resonant with the consequences of Genesis. We have been born into significance. That is creation.

God's work of creation is a song that He sings into being. Creation is a work of art that is not required but is better for being. It adds nothing to God, since adding to God is outside the realm of possibility, yet He takes pleasure in it. So we would say with the twenty-four elders in Revelation 4:11, "Thou art worthy, O Lord, to receive glory and honor and power: for thou hast created all things, and for thy pleasure they are and were created" (KJV).

Prior to God's making of it, there was no absence of the universe. There can be no absence of anything that has no existence. Prior to God's act of creation, there was no need for the universe. Yet in His exuberance, in His joy, God worked; and the resulting work, though it is not required, has immediate significance.

God's Work: Expressing His Being

As a painting expresses something of the nature of the artist who created it, so the universe expresses the nature of God. In describing the divinity of Jesus Christ, the following Scripture ties the nature of God to that of creation.

He is the image of the invisible God, the first-born of all creation; for in him all things were created, in heaven and on earth, visible and invisible, whether thrones or dominions or principalities or authorities—all things were created through him and for him. He is before all things, and in him all things hold together (Col. 1:15–17 RSV).

Thus we see the work of creation, an expression of His being. That leads us to the next question, which is whether that is also true for man. Does man's work express his being? One would suspect so, based on the fact that we are created in God's image and can be expected to parallel His being. But we have a

concrete example in Adam, since he gives us a picture of man
prior to the Fall.

Adam—His Being—His Work

Adam. We can picture him when he opened his eyes at the
dawn of his creation. The first thoughts that filled his con-
sciousness were of the One who breathed the breath of life into
him. The created looked into the being of the Creator with
spiritual eyes totally free from the opacity of sin.

Adam saw in God such radiant beauty that being in itself was
an all-sufficient delight. From our perspective, he might have
questioned his reason for being, but the object of his vision
authenticated Himself and Adam's experience simultaneously.
Questions about meaning and purpose were absurd and incon-
ceivable at the time. He simply delighted in being.

How was Adam's being expressed? The answer is quite clear
in the Book of Genesis. "The LORD God took the man, and put
him into the garden of Eden to dress it and to keep it" (Gen.
2:15 KJV).

In this role, Adam took his specific place in the interrelated
scheme of creation. There was a particular place for him in the
garden. He kept order and balance in Eden. He worked!
Though Adam's job had practical results, the ultimate significance of what he did was tied to the significance of creation
itself. Creation as God's work is expressive of His being. For
Adam to act and operate effectively was to experience the
significance of being.

Adam exerted himself in the constant awareness that he had
looked into the eyes of God and as a product of God's work had
come to know in what spirit, with what grace, he ought to till the
ground. He knew that love's eyes were upon his work. What a
delight it must have been for Adam to cultivate the ground for
the pleasure of God! God's pleasure was Adam's pleasure, and
both pleasures were attained through work.

The curse of the Fall is not that we have to work, but that we have to work by the sweat of the brow. Work is no longer a pure expression of being, it is contaminated with the laborious requirement to take care of our physical needs. We become preoccupied with toil and wages, and we exist in a spiritual blindness that cuts us off from the vision Adam was conscious of in the garden.

Comparing Adam's situation to that of the contemporary Christian, we wonder if it is possible for us to capture vision and knowledge. Now that we have been restored to fellowship with God, can our everyday work become, to some degree, the equivalent of Adam's tilling the garden—a pleasure, a delight, and meaningful?

Scripture proclaims the answer is yes, but we must be realistic in our enthusiasm. Adam was in a setting that constantly displayed the harmony of God's creation. Adam also had the spiritual eyes to see and know his place in it. He knew work was good.

We are estranged from God's creation and do not know our place in it. We are in a fallen creation that doesn't encourage optimism about the worth of work. This is where faith steps in and enables us to be hopeful in our place of work. It is a matter of trusting the message of the Book of Genesis, what we here call the Genesis Principle.

The Genesis Principle

The Genesis Principle is the fundamental, biblical conclusion that creation is a good work regardless of what happened to it in the eventual Fall of man. The scriptural declaration of God's opinion in the Book of Genesis is a foundational attitude toward creation that we who are adopted into the family of God must share. Remember that God was making His positive statement from His eternal perspective. He was not looking at a static moment in history and giving it His approval, but was "anticipating" the eventual Fall and restoration of creation. God knew in those bold strokes of bringing time, space, and matter into existence that they were the stage for the being of man, who would fall so despairingly low, apparently beyond the possibility of hope.

Out of that seeming tragedy, however, God spun salvation by grace, whereby man is taken beyond Eden to be adopted into the family of God. Knowing that inspires worship. It can also have practical consequences as we live our daily lives in this strange world—strange because it is simultaneously a wonderful place and a horrible place.

The world is full of beauty, yet with dreadful frequency people have longed for death as private tragedies, war, or famine have overtaken them. Incomprehensible pain and sorrow have accompanied man's trek through the centuries. The world can be a bleak place to live in.

How do we live reasonably when the world pushes us to schizoid existence? How do we maintain equilibrium in such outrageous extremes? Thousands cannot and millions plod on, hoping that somehow it will turn out all right.

The Christian has more than a vague optimism around which he gathers his hopes, however. He participates in the life of Christ, whose experience of tragedy surpasses that of any other man. Life in Christ is a reconciled life in which we do not let troubles blind us to beauty and in which beauty does not distract us from living through sorrows.

As Christ endured the cross for the sake of the joy set before Him, so we in like manner are to endure our trials. May we be delivered from a distorted pietism that would have us take pleasure in pain. But let us address pain with our eye on the end of the story. Let us exult in the eventual victory that is ours even while we are in the battle.

The Genesis Principle places a smile on the lips of the Christian as he faces his work and culture, knowing *his place in them*. It enables appreciation of work and culture as God's inventions. It allows a Christian to look at the distortion brought into work and culture by Lucifer with the knowledge that God anticipated such perversion in Genesis and planned redemption. Such knowledge allows each individual to take his place in creation and become who God designed him to be in spite of all difficulties. God Himself is behind that creative intention for each of us. We must align ourselves with His creative purpose and utilize the abilities He has given us. This way we become living demonstrations of God's creativity, and we confidently apply ourselves to the purposes God has for the world.

5

The Gifts of God
for the People of God

AS WITH ADAM, GOD EQUIPS ALL MANKIND WITH gifts in untold measure and variety with which to subdue and have dominion over the world. When matched to roles suitable to those gifts, good work is produced. One endowed with a gift who has used it for the benefit of others receives the rich, deeply satisfying reward experienced by those who give of what God has given them.

God has given the gifts. There is no way in which a person who does not have a particular gift can develop it on his own. Human beings can only exercise the gifts God has originally given, and in doing so they have the terrible choice of exercising them for good or for evil. The exercise of those gifts makes possible civilizations and kingdoms, earthly or heavenly.

Thou didst ascend the high mount, leading captives in thy train, and receiving gifts among men, even among the rebellious, that the LORD God may dwell there. Blessed be the Lord, who daily bears us up; God is our salvation (Psalm 68:18, 19 RSV).

If we examine the lives of famous people, Christian and non-Christian, we find their success depended on the use they made of their gifts. Leonardo da Vinci, George Washington Carver, Martin Luther, John D. Rockefeller, Thomas Edison, Thomas Jefferson, and Billy Graham, just to name a few—all achieved what they achieved through the use of certain gifts within themselves.

Most of us can readily affirm that principle in the case of the "superstars," but we are not consciously aware that the world figuratively revolves around *all* the good gifts given to man. All the following have only been possible because of men and women using gifts with which they were endowed: every advance in knowledge; every sound decision; every invention; every prosperous community; every beautiful poem; every righteous crusade; every profitable enterprise; every sumptuous apple pie; every lovely song; every effective merchandising concept; every new tool; every new method; every new process; every moving speech; every world's record; every hard sale; every beautiful garden; every pleasing design; every home run; every great painting; every important legal document; every major advance in civilization.

Check the biography of any famous chef, business executive, revolutionary, chemist, architect, cross-country skier, jazz buff, or ham radio engineer and you will encounter the same fact: the outstanding performance was achieved through certain "natural" gifts possessed by the person.

What is true at a national level is true within your county, where the person who is known for intricate, homemade quilts, for consistently winning the prize for the best watermelon pickles, for raising the finest hog, or for producing the largest crop yield has achieved success based on certain special gifts. You may remember from your youth certain kids were stars in spelling or math; one usually took home all the marbles; one was always elected an officer; another was the high scorer, the long-ball hitter, the best dresser, or the gang leader. Each superlative performance was based on gifts.

In whatever community you live, there are certain people whose contribution is outstanding and whose gifts are apparent—a scoutmaster, a doctor, a store owner, a choir director, a Mr. Fix-It, a mother of six fine boys, one who runs community affairs, or the person who is always there when needed.

Wherever you work, some people stand out. Certain people seem very gifted at selling, cutting costs, managing the company, getting things done or running a well-organized shop.

Certain people are the ones you go to when you have a job with a specially close tolerance, when you need someone to cut through the red tape, or when you have to make sure all the loose ends are tied up. All these are stars in their own world and do well because of their gifts.

Successful Organizations Based on the Gifts of Their Members

Moving from the individual to the organization, we see the same principle in force. Successful organizations are successful as a result of the exercise of gifts possessed by certain of their employees. Whether the bottom line is profit or mission accomplished, the principle is the same.

Why do you suppose a certain organization is noteworthy for its service, one for the soundness and integrity of its product, another for its labor relations? The reason is people who are gifted at what they do.

Why a particular department hums in quiet efficiency, why the northwest sales territory always leads the nation, why particular products are requested, why an organization's entry into new markets is so timely and well thought-out—are all traceable to certain gifted people in jobs suitable for those gifts.

Looking behind the organizational veil, we see the person who always meets deadlines, one who consistently generates action, the supervisor who moves like General Patton in an emergency, and the union leader whom both sides trust and listen to.

Closer to home is home. The complex, demanding jobs of wife, mother, counselor, organizer, chef, servant, maintenance mechanic, manager, interior decorator, and disciplinarian do not find responding gifts in one person. But if any one or more of those elements is performed well, God's gifts are involved, and in that area the woman experiences profound joy in her work. The same is true for any man taking a similar role at home.

What is true of the successful factory, bank, school, or home is also true of the successful church. Regardless of how one measures such success, the church that is successful does well because of God-given gifts placed suitably and functioning properly.

The reason for our emphasis and reemphasis on this point is that we hope to dispel a distorted view most Christians have of the worldly activities of business, education, arts, and leisure. Many Christians believe that such activities are worldly, meaning they are solely the products of man's endeavors. It is no wonder there is so much guilt among highly committed Christians who with that perspective must conclude that only those activities connected with Christian ministry are worth pursuit.

Behind this distorted view is a monumental error, namely, the attributing to man the ability to create concepts of organization, economics, science, communication, and creativity on his own as if they were not discoveries of principles ordained by God. Civilization is only possible because of God and is not in any remote sense an independent development of man.

Man cannot develop anything original. He must use what God has provided. As shown earlier, he cannot even sin without using a good. Behind every sin there is a God-given good. Gluttony is a distortion of the pleasure of eating. God is the one who invented tastes and the tongue to savor them. Fornication is possible because God created sexual pleasure and the physiology to produce that pleasure. Hate is possible because of the potentials of relationships, which surely have a divine source. Nothing man does can be done without physical and mental capacities created by God, working on concepts or materials also created by God. (This truth allows one to see how hideous sin really is. We take that which is good, true, and beautiful and pervert it, then hand it over to Satan to rule.)

Civilization was the goal of Eden. Adam and Eve were to be fruitful, to replenish the earth and subdue it (see Gen. 1:28), not merely to carry on as custodians of a mini-agrarian society. Being fruitful meant the eventual development of families, tribes, countries, and jurisdictions. That in turn would require increasingly sophisticated methods of communication, which would be developed by those who had the gift to deal with symbols and develop the technologies required as a parallel advance.

If it were not for man's pride and subsequent Fall, these discoveries would have been made without the agonizingly slow progression that has characterized man's history from the first written symbol to the efficiency of modern communication. They also would have been made without the inaccuracies and inadequacies that have plagued communications for centuries. Further, they would have been discovered without the potential of their being used to communicate evil ideas, or for purposes of war. The fact that they are so used, however, does not permit us to say that communications are bad in themselves.

The same can be said for business and industry. It is unnecessary to point out the obvious evils that have emerged from both areas. Those evils, however, come about not because business and industry are evil by nature, but because business can be exploited to serve greed. Business and industry do not produce greed. The sick nature of man does. Consider what beauty there would be if unfallen man conducted business and manufacturing enterprises. Can you imagine the wonder of people making beautiful products that have integrity of design and purpose, and then those products being distributed by way of ingenious systems to all those in need of the products? Can you imagine people involved in all phases of those activities doing what they are gifted to do under God's authority?

The world has little conception of such business, but the Christian should. And he should take his place in the current systems of business, industry, communication, science, politics, education, and so on with the power and conviction that rightfully accompany one who knows God and is armed with God's gifts to give witness to what should take place universally.

Look at the complexity of creation and see how each cell, microorganism, plant, and animal functions in a vastly intricate ecological system. Though we realize that it is a fallen creation and that the lamb has yet to lie down with the lion, we do not allow that fact to diminish our praise to the Maker of such wondrous work. That is evident in centuries of Christian and Jewish devotional outpouring in art, literature, and music that has used the themes of nature. Mountains, trees, birds, sky, and stars are all part of the celebration of the wonder of creation, *even though they belong to a fallen creation*. Some day it will be a redeemed nature we will view. Hope in that reality serves to enhance our view of nature as it appears to us now.

Why not have the same view of civilization? Why not assume that the new Jerusalem will function through the use of gifts, including those of government and administration? "Do you not know that the saints will judge the world?" (1 Cor. 6:2 RSV).

The material resources of nature are needed by man to build civilization, to bless him individually, and to bring about communities. That is why we believe the subject of work and job-fit is so important. If nature is not irrelevant (and we do not see how the Christian could think it is), then all the implications we have drawn from it require us to believe that neither is civilization. And if civilization is important, our place in it is also. That place is our job. We do not believe it is possible for Christians to treat this lightly without seriously diminishing personal joy and Christian witness.

Viewing the vocational disaster the world has produced in that three or four out of every five people are in the wrong jobs (according to a study released by the Marketing & Research Corp. of Princeton, N.J., in 1976), we as Christians should abhor any possibility that we would produce the same poisonous fruit. What a mission field! If you want to see a potentially major weapon for good in God's Kingdom, we would like to portray him for you:

He is the person whose work fits his gifts and who demonstrates the harmony between man and work that God intends for His people.

He enjoys his work and can be affirmed in it, and he thereby becomes attractive to the people around him.

He knows his gift comes from the Lord and is not of his making, so he visibly shows the grace of God in his life and gives God the praise.

He knows that even if he is working for a secular business, the

principles by which that business has any cohesion at all are
God's creation. And he knows that all the distortion of God's
purpose expressed by that particular business cannot dim the
reality that no God means no business.

He does not need to overreact to fluctuations of market and
economy, because he is in God's hands and God will bring
about systems that are not transient and do not decay.

He shows glimpses of his ultimate purpose by an authoritative demonstration of meaning in his job, in the day he has, with
his faculties, with a sense of satisfaction.

He ignores the systems of the world that would have him
decide on his place according to their measures of fame, pres-
tige, money, and success. He does not lust after what does not
fit who he is, even if it is good for others.

He has thought through his place in his family and society
and is able to say or show who he is. He does not waste years
trying to discover himself in vain career experiments.

He assumes the disciplines of better craftsmanship, whether
through schooling, study, or practice.

He knows that God has His eye on his work.

He is visibly calm in the midst of any storm around him.

He allies himself with products or services of integrity.

He affirms others where they produce craftsmanship.

He measures success not by how high or low he is in terms of
position, but by how well he does the work he is gifted to do.

Unlike the transient joy experienced by someone who does
not know the Lord, the Christian can approach work that requires his gifts as a holy task, with commitment, zeal, and
delight.

Integrating his faith in his work can bring an infusion of new
vitality to both faith and work. Knowing that work lies at the
center of his calling will enliven his faith and revive a sense of
gratitude, which in turn will draw him closer to the Lord.

When you know you are neither the source of your gifts nor
the one ultimately responsible for the impact they make, you are
talking about real freedom, real joy, real worship. Abiding in
Christ can become a reality for all Christians who felt it was

unavailable up to now because they believed their work was of the world, as if they could separate a portion of their lives from divine influence.

We repeat: every act or event in your personal or organizational life that you would describe as outstanding is the result of a God-given gift. Whether your success is making satisfying meals on a tight budget; timely business decisions; affordable new products that meet real needs; oil poured on troubled waters; a new time-saving system; or a labor-saving improvement, the principle is the same. Each action comes because men and women used the gifts they were given to use.

Much has been accomplished during the course of history despite our fallen state. But think about how much more could be done if we were all doing work that made proper use of our God-given gifts! Think of the joy and fulfillment we would know as individuals!

6

Discovering Your Design

IN RECENT YEARS, INCREASING NUMBERS OF people have asked "Who am I?"—a question that on the surface seems a bit sophomoric and another example of the self-centeredness so much in vogue. Of course, what is actually being expressed is quite serious and real and is ultimately concerned with giving rather than receiving. Were the feelings behind the question better articulated, they would probably appear as, "What is my purpose? What do I have to offer the world? What am I made to do?"

It is one thing to wax enthusiastic over the gifts God has given to each of us and another to deal with the obvious problem of identifying those gifts. The world, for all its sophisticated technologies, has not done too well in this area, as job-fit statistics show. There is a method, however, that enables people to get at the answers to those questions so they can arrive' at a basic understanding of what gifts they have been given. They can use that understanding for planning their place in life. In this chapter, we want to explain the method to you.

A key to unlocking this method is found in an intriguing verse from the Book of Galatians. There God exhorts us through the apostle Paul to pay special attention to our achievements: "Each man should examine his own conduct for himself; then he can measure his achievement by comparing himself with himself and not with anyone else" (6:4 NEB). This verse can be seen merely as an affirmation of individuality, but it is also the means for understanding the uniqueness of who we are and what we have been given to give.

[handwritten annotations: Galatians 6:4 — Affirmation of Individuality — Uniqueness of who we are and what distinguishes us]

A History Lesson

To "measure your achievement" requires an appreciation of biblical history and an understanding of your own personal history. History is an important factor in discovering the will of God for mankind. Large portions of the Bible are given over to history, enabling us to discover the pattern of God's intentions. With a review of that history, we can perceive His character and the place and purpose of men and women as they responded to it.

Likewise history is important in discovering the will of God for the individual. You may view your history as bad, good, or both. And you may be right in your judgment. However, we can use your history because God's design of you and your gifts is revealed in it. *[handwritten: Personal History – God Design of you]*

The contents of your personal history are not random or accidental. Your unique personality, character, and talents have done much to shape the important events in your life. There is a clear, strong connection between who you are and what you have done. Your own design, or makeup, has been a driving force in thousands of situations and, for good or ill, has plainly revealed itself. You may or may not be pleased with the way you carried out your design, but at least be pleased that you are God's handiwork (see Eph. 2:10) and have been designed with specific gifts and a motivation to use those gifts.

As suggested by the apostle Paul, you begin to find God's design of you by identifying achievements that give you a sense of joy or satisfaction when used in a particular way for certain purposes. This may be a questionable technique for those who have had to deal with the negatives of sin in their lives, especially sin that has cloaked itself as good. We have found, however, that sin is less related to the exercise of our gifts and more related to exercising our egos as if we had created our talents. *[handwritten margin notes: You find God's design of you]*

Identifying Your Design

When we write about gifts and motivations, we do not merely mean talent. Talent is included, but we mean something far

Motivational Pattern   *Likes & Dislikes*

more fundamental. In our professional experience, evaluating thousands of individuals over twenty years, we have found that each person displays an entire behavioral system, which we call a "motivational pattern," over and over again. In other words, we all have individual likes and dislikes. We react to people, things, and circumstances in the same way time and again. We human beings are far more consistent in our thoughts, words and actions than we realize. Thus we say such things as "Isn't that just like him?"

The motivational pattern is evidence that God has designed us not as haphazard collections of possibilities, but as people with highly detailed gifts that differ from one individual to another. Those gifts emerge from the depths of our motives and determine our place in the scheme of things. As each animal and organism functions in a particular place in God's creation, so we, too, are designed for a particular role in the human community and in the world.

By this we do not mean that we must fatalistically obey a pattern implanted in us somewhere, but that there is a style to who we are. We are not shapeless. We have a mode of action, a certain way of operating that is unique to us and that calls us to be what we were made to be, not what others want us to be.

Elements of Your Design

To give you a feel for the nature of a motivational pattern, here are its elements:

- A central motivational thrust, or outcome you are motivated to achieve
- Certain motivated abilities you are motivated to use
- Certain subject matter you are motivated to work with or through
- Certain circumstances within which you are motivated to operate
- A certain way you are motivated to relate to and operate with others

Now let's look at each element of the pattern in more detail.

1. Central motivational thrust

An examination of a person's enjoyable achievements will reveal a common thread (for which the person always strives) tying together all the things he does well. For convenience, we identify this thread under the label "central motivational thrust." Out of the apparent diversity of what a person has done, this central motivational thrust emerges as the single overriding and unifying factor.

For one person it may be meeting needs and requirements; for another it may be overcoming obstacles and persevering against difficulties. For someone else the central motivational thrust might be serving and helping other people. For still another, it could be building and developing things. For someone else it might be gaining recognition, honor and awards, and so on.

To give a concrete example, let's examine the apostle Paul's central motivational thrust, which was to prevail.

Paul — prevailed

Prevailing against Christians

Saul, still breathing threats and murder against the disciples of the Lord, went to the high priest and asked him for letters to the synagogues at Damascus, so that if he found any belonging to the Way, men or women, he might bring them bound to Jerusalem (Acts 9:1, 2 RSV).

Prevailing against Jews

"He has come here for this purpose, to bring them bound before the chief priests." But Saul increased all the more in strength, and confounded the Jews who lived in Damascus by proving that Jesus was the Christ (Acts 9:21, 22 RSV).

Prevailing in debate

Preaching boldly in the name of the Lord. And he spoke and disputed against the Hellenists (Acts 9:29 RSV).

Prevailing against fellow believers

And when Paul and Barnabas had no small dissension and debate with them, Paul and Barnabas and some of the others were appointed to go up to Jerusalem to the apostles and the elders about this question (Acts 15:2 RSV).

Prevailing against anybody

So he argued in the synagogue with the Jews and the devout persons, and in the market place every day with those who chanced to be there (Acts 17:17 RSV).

Prevailing in the synagogue

And he entered the synagogue and for three months spoke boldly, arguing and pleading about the kingdom of God; but when some were stubborn and disbelieved, speaking evil of the Way before the congregation, he withdrew from them, taking the disciples with him, and argued daily in the hall of Tyrannus (Acts 19:8, 9 RSV).

Other Scriptures also display that "I will win out" quality. Paul boasted (albeit for the sake of others) that he was beaten more than others and in prison more than others. He described himself as running a race, and he urged us to do the same. He repeatedly used the metaphor of the race, urging us to gain the laurel, win the crown.

Paul operated in a clearly consistent way, and oddly enough, not in a way that looks so saintly, given many a Christian's view of saintliness. Without that strong, prevailing element called Paul, however, the church would never have gotten started.

2. Certain motivated abilities

Through their achievements, individuals show their ways of getting things done. These include such abilities as:

persuading the boss	conceiving ideas
writing reports	negotiating and bargaining
analyzing problems	teaching children
designing a widget	organizing work

Achievements reveal 5 to 8 abilities that occur frequently!

Examining any person's achievement experiences will yield five to eight abilities that recur frequently. Those abilities are the ones that person is particularly motivated to use. That is, they are the abilities both that he is *able* to use and that he *wants* to use.

One person is good at planning and building, another at designing and creating; one is good at investigating and bargaining, another at experimenting and evaluating; one person is good at speaking and motivating, another at operating and maintaining; and so forth. In each case, what the person enjoys and is good at is a result of how God made him. As God said when arranging the construction of the wilderness tabernacle, "I have given to all able men ability" (Ex. 31:6 RSV). People have more abilities than motivated abilities, but the use of the latter is their area of strength. The use of motivated abilities is rarely boring given the right context.

3. Certain subject matter

People get satisfaction over and over again by dealing with their favorite subject matter. Here are just a very few examples of subject matters that people like:

- Figures usually are present.
- Money is frequently involved.
- Work is in great detail.
- In many cases, a method is developed.
- People are central to most achievements.
- Things of a mechanical nature are worked on.

Examining achievement experiences will yield three to five subject matters that recur frequently. Those subjects reveal the content, the objects, the mechanisms with which that person is motivated to work.

Because you will attempt to shape or even distort your job or role, consciously or unconsciously, to include your favorite subject matter, it is critical that your work require or at least accommodate those subjects.

The Lord was mindful of that fact when He called attention to certain people He had created to work with certain subject matter:

He has filled him with divine spirit, making him skilful and ingenious, expert in every craft, and a master of design, whether in gold, silver, and copper, or cutting precious stones for setting, or carving wood. . . . He has inspired . . . workers and designers of every kind, engravers, seamsters, embroiderers in violet, purple, and scarlet yarn and fine linen, and weavers, fully endowing them with skill to execute all kinds of work (Ex. 34:31–33, 35 NEB).

4. Certain circumstances

People seek certain circumstances that they enjoy. If they cannot find them, frequently they will try to make them. Examples include these kinds of circumstances:

- Stress or competition is usually present.
- The situation is structured and defined.
- The situation is unstructured and fluid.
- Things are "projectized" and have a clear beginning and end.
- Problems are frequently involved.

Some people rise to full height when asked to help. Some want crusades to join or a Goliath to face before they are motivated. Others need a group situation in which to work. There are still others who seek to do things requiring an immediate response to demands. Others must have plenty of time to get their act together before they step out.

Knowing those differences between His children, God told Gideon how to identify those motivated by combat and battle:

"Now make a proclamation for all the people to hear, that anyone who is scared or frightened is to leave Mount Gilead at once and go back home." Twenty-two thousand of them went, and ten thousand were left. The LORD then said to Gideon, "There are still too many. Bring them down to the water, and I will separate them for you there. When I say to you, 'This man shall go with you', he shall go; and if I say, 'This man shall not go with you', he shall not go." . . . The LORD said to Gideon, "With the three hundred men who lapped I will save you and deliver Midian into your hands, and all the rest may go home" (Judg. 7:3, 4,7 TEV).

The Lord didn't use anyone just because he was a soldier. He didn't select according to spiritual maturity. He selected those who revealed by their behavior that their gift was to be the kind of soldiers who would produce victory.

5. A certain way of relating to and operating with others

In their achievements, people reveal a characteristic way of relating with others. By examining the achievements of a person, the following conclusions can be reached:

- Frequently put in the position of a leader.
- Always operated pretty much on their own.
- Consistently part of a team effort.
- Concerned with influencing others, but had no direct authority over those influenced.
- Usually managed a group independently of directions from higher authority.

No part of the pattern is more critical than how the person is motivated to operate with people. This area of our design is the reason for so much distortion, confusion, imbalance, and fleshliness in the Body of Christ and in all denominations, particularly those with relatively little governing structure.

Scripture abounds in references to specific roles we are to fulfill in relation to one another. "The gifts we possess differ as they are allotted to us by God's grace, and must be exercised accordingly: . . . the gift of administration, in administration. . . . if you are a leader, exert yourself to lead" (Rom. 12:6,7,8 NEB). That instruction is as clear as possible. We are to take our roles in working relations with others, according to the gifts God has given. It is a serious error to assume that just because we have demonstrated excellent performance in one role, we can therefore expect to produce excellence in any role.

"Take you wise men, and understanding, and known among your tribes, and I will make them rulers over you" (Deut. 1:13

KJV). Again the principle is simple. If you need wise men with understanding to be rulers, take the ones who have demonstrated those gifts. Consistency of performance in the past is the best predictor of future performance. We see the same principle in the life of Joseph in Egypt: "And his master saw that the LORD was with him, and that the LORD made all that he did to prosper in his hand. . . . and he made him overseer over his house" (Gen. 39:3,4 KJV). Note that prosperity did not come automatically (Joseph had a term in jail), but the Lord eventually did bless that to which Joseph applied his gifts. Potiphar was smart enough to make Joseph overseer because he had already demonstrated success. Later on, those same gifts were used by the Pharaoh for the benefit of the entire nation.

The Details of Your Design

The various segments of the motivational pattern, or design, just outlined represent only a skeleton. Careful examination of your enjoyable achievements will reveal rich evidence of who you are.

Each element of each part of the pattern has a particular quality. For example, a person may have an ability to teach, but mainly by demonstration rather than by lecturing. A person may work better one-on-one rather than with a group. A person can manage others but wants to stay involved in the action. Another is motivated to learn about new things if he can experience the learning in some hands-on, experimental fashion. Someone is motivated to build things, but you notice he is one-of-a-kind—he never makes the same thing twice. A person is really good at giving talks and presentations, but only after mastering the subject and carefully preparing what to say. Or someone loves to be in a debate, particularly when he can just improvise on the spot.

The existence of such a design may be a foreign idea to you. However, after many years of helping people in churches, schools, and corporations discover their designs, we have yet to find even one individual who did not evidence a complete motivational pattern, nor have we ever found one person's pattern to exactly duplicate another's. Such extensive experience forces us to assume confidently that each person who reads this book also has a unique design.

Recalling Your Joys

Biographical Form

Now that you've come this far, see how much of your own motivational pattern you can identify. Recalling as many of your enjoyable achievement experiences as you can, fill out the biographical form located in the appendix to this book. Instructions and examples are contained in the form, so you should have no trouble understanding the kind and amount of detail needed to describe your enjoyable achievement experiences.

Having completed your own list of achievement experiences in the biographical form, try your hand at identifying the elements of your motivational pattern. The next few pages contain the steps to be used in discerning a motivational pattern from your achievements. You will need to review the achievement data more than once.

The lists of motivational elements we provide below are not meant to be exhaustive. We keep discovering new additions to our own lists, so a "final" version does not seem possible. (God has created infinite variety in man!) It is also so extensive that it would be far too ponderous to be helpful here.

What we have done is to compile those elements that will allow you to get a large hold on self-understanding and not attempt to duplicate the detail we would provide professionally.

Identifying the Central Motivational Thrust

Step 1   Using the samples below, examine your achievements (using the SIMA biographical form in the appendix) for a common thread that either matches one of these or can be expressed similarly. You will probably be able to find a key phrase in the language you used that essentially describes the central thrust or result you are attempting to discern.

Acquire/possess—money/material things/status/people
Wants to have own baby, to own toys, bicycles, houses, furniture, and family.

Be in charge/command—others/things/organization
Wants to be on top, in authority, in the saddle, where it can be determined how things will be done.

Combat/prevail—over adversaries/evil/opposing philosophies
Wants to come against the bad guys, entrenched status quo, old technology.

Develop/build—structures/technical things
Wants to make something where there was nothing.

Excel/be the best—versus others/conventional standards
Wants to be the fastest, first, longest, earliest, biggest, most complicated, better than others.

Exploit/achieve potential—situations/markets/things/people
Sees a silk purse, a giant talent, a hot product, a promising market before the fact.

Gain response/influence behavior—from people/through people
Wants dogs, cats, people, and groups to react to his touch.

Gain recognition/attention—from peers/public authority
Wants to wave at the cheering crowd, appear in the paper, be known, dance in the spotlight.

Improve/make better—self/others/work/organizations
Makes what is marginal, good; what is good, better; what makes a little money, make a lot of money.

Make the team/grade—established by others/by system
Gains access to the varsity, Eagle Scout rank, the Silver Circle, the country club, the executive dining room.

Meet needs/fulfill expectations—demanded/needed/inherent
Strives to meet specifications, shipping schedules, what the customer wants, what the boss has expressed.

Make work/make effective—things/systems/operations
Fixes what is broken, changes what is out-of-date, redesigns what was poorly conceived.

Master/perfect—subject/skill/equipment/objects
Goes after rough edges, complete domination of a technique, control over the variables.

Organize and operate—business/team/product line
Wants to be an entrepreneur, the beginner of new businesses.

Overcome/persevere—obstacles/handicaps/unknown/odds
Goes after hungry tigers with a pop gun, concave mountains with slippery boots.

Pioneer/explore—technology/cultures/ideas
Presses through established lines, knowledge, boundaries.

Serve/help—people/organizations/causes
Carries the soup, ministers to the wounded, helps those in need.

Shape/influence—material/policy/people
Wants to leave a mark, to cause change, to make an impact.
What is your central motivational thrust? Write it out below.

_____

Now prove it! Support your conclusion with evidence from your achievements.
(For example, acquire/possess: Made a big haul at Christmas. Purchased auto at age 16. Built up cash reserves. Completely remodeled interior of house. Achieved large income as broker.)

_____

_____

_____

_____

Identifying Motivated Abilities

Step 2   Extract and write down all verbs that denote actions performed while you were doing each achievement (use the SIMA form).

Step 3   Group the verbs together that fall within the following groupings, but try not to identify more than six or seven. If you believe you have more, determine the five to eight most central to doing what was important to you.

- An *investigative* ability: interview, experiment
- A *learning* ability: observe, research, study, practice
- A *visualizing* ability: conceptualize, picture, dream
- An *evaluating* ability: analyze, assess, select
- A *formulating* ability: theorize, define
- A *planning* ability: design, lay out, schedule, strategize
- A *creating* ability: invent, improvise, innovate, paint
- An *organizing* ability: collect, synthesize, systematize
- A *developing* ability: improve, tinker, modify
- A *constructing* ability: build, assemble, put together
- An *operating* ability: manage, administer, manipulate
- An *implementing* ability: do physically, execute
- A *counseling* ability: coach, advise
- A *supervising* ability: lead, coordinate, direct
- A *performing* ability: act, demonstrate, dance, speak
- A *teaching* ability: train, instruct, explain, demonstrate
- A *writing* ability: edit, compose, advertise
- An *influencing* ability: convince, advocate, motivate, sell

The abilities have a general chronology that is helpful when assembling them into groupings; that is, there is generally a logical order of events followed.

List five to eight abilities you identified.

_____

_____

_____

_____

_____

_____

_____

_____

Now prove the presence of each ability by citing evidence for it from your achievements. (For example, analyze/evaluate: Made extensive cost studies. Evaluated the data. Analyzed our burlap profit. Analyzed the company's selling area.)

1. Ability: _____

   Evidence: _____

   _____

   _____

   _____

2. Ability: _____

   Evidence: _____

   _____

   _____

   _____

3. Ability: _____

   Evidence: _____

   _____

   _____

   _____

4. Ability: _____

   Evidence: _____

   _____

   _____

   _____

5. Ability: _____

   Evidence: _____

   _____

   _____

   _____

6. Ability: _____

   Evidence: _____

   _____

   _____

Identifying Motivated Subject Matter
and Circumstances

Step 4 From the achievement information, extract and write down the nouns that are related to the actions involved when you are doing each achievement. Those nouns will describe the kinds of objects and mechanisms you are motivated to work with or through. They will also describe the situations, circumstances, or context within which you are motivated to work.

Assemble those nouns in groups that denote similar objects or circumstances, as illustrated by the samples below in the categories. These are only examples.

The *objects* you work with:

- figures/details
- living things
- physical/structural things
- projects/programs
- things/hardware/equipment
- words/language/symbols
- people/relationships

The *mechanisms* you work through:

- art/design
- controls/budgets/schedules
- ideas/concepts
- enterprise/business
- systems/methods
- policy/strategy

Now prove the existence of these elements of your pattern by citing evidence from your achievements. (For example, projects/programs and systems/methods: Designed a new distribution system that cut shipping costs. Streamlined the family budget. Developed a new sales program that reduces company travel costs.)

Object, mechanism, subject matter: _____

Evidence: _____

_____

_____

_____

Object, mechanism, subject matter: _____

Evidence: _____

_____

_____

_____

Object, mechanism, subject matter: _____

Evidence: _____

_____

_____

_____

Object, mechanism, subject matter: _____

Evidence: _____

_____

_____

Object, mechanism, subject matter: _____

Evidence: _____

_____

_____

_____

Identifying the Motivated Relation with Others

How you operate with others is determined by examining the active role you maintain in relation to others who may be involved when you perform your achievements.

Step 5 Examine your list of achievements for statements that indicate the way you relate to others.

Step 6 Extract phrases that describe the relationship.

Step 7 Study those phrases that state your relationship with others, and find the best fit from the following:

Team Member —Must operate in the company of others.
—Contribution merged with efforts of others.

Individualist —Content to operate with others or by himself.
—Wants role and contribution defined and traceable to his efforts.
—Wants to be able to secure results primarily through his efforts.

Team Leader —Involved with subordinates in the action.
—Influences their actions by example or expertise.
—While leading, may still tend to be preoccupied with his personal tasks.

Coordinator —Often causes others to take action who are not required to report to him.
—Prefers to operate without hire-fire or confronting authority.

Director   —Directs the actions of others to perform
                   exactly his way.
                  —Gets involved at the level of detail.
                  —Uses people as extensions of himself.

Manager   —Manages the talents of others to bring about
                   a result.
                  —Normally allows others to determine how
                   they will perform.
                  —May tend to delegate authority and respon-
                   sibility while still maintaining overall con-
                   trol.

Coach   —Develops others' talents in supportive role.
                  —Does not normally participate in action.
                  —Does not focus on or control outcome/result.

What was your predominant relationship with others?

_____

_____

   Support your conclusion by citing evidence from your
achievements.
(For example, team member: With consulting engineers rede-
signed electrical service. Together with cousin repaired car.
Worked with father and carpenter and built 2-room addition to
house. Planned together with plant superintendent renovation
of existing facilities.)

_____

_____

_____

_____

_____

_____

Discovering your motivated abilities in the above exercise is not a matter of focusing on where you happen to be today in your development. Using achievements from as early as you can remember to the present demonstrates that we are not taking an inventory of transient factors. (If you want a more detailed treatment of how to use the SIMA method, we suggest you look at our earlier book, _The Truth about You_.)

Pattern Characteristics

Having gained a rough idea of the elements of your motivational pattern, let's look now at three important characteristics of that pattern. Your motivational pattern plays such a dominant role in how you live your life because it (1) is permanent, (2) is consistent, and (3) controls your behavior. We will consider each of these in turn.

"For the gifts and the call of God are irrevocable" (Rom. 11:29 RSV). This verse refers to the call of God to Israel and cannot be used to prove the principle of a permanent pattern here. It does, however, introduce how God can operate in the matter of gifts and calling. It becomes startling when we discover in our work that achievements at age forty are only more complex manifestations of the same pattern revealed at age twelve.

- The child repairing a robin's wing at age seven is giving intravenous injections to her diabetic husband at age thirty and is hustling opposition to increased teacher-pupil ratios at age forty-five.
- The child acquiring his first scooter car when he is four, his first bicycle at nine, his first car at sixteen, and his first

house at age thirty is still acquiring money or material things at age sixty.

- The child defending his sister against a bully at age eight is preoccupied at age twenty-nine with his ministry to people facing personal tragedy or death and is conquering and making friends with inner-city gang leaders at age forty-five.

Those examples, taken from our files, indicate the enduring nature of people's designs. People do not lose the gifts they have been given or acquire a new set at any point in life. God does not change His mind about His creation of each individual.

This must be understood in the context of growth. We should grow consistently in Christ, blossoming and bearing fruit and becoming more like what He has designed us to be with each passing year. To illustrate, while we can say that an oak seedling is the same as a forty-year-old oak, we can also state that in some way the latter is *more* an oak. Similarly, each person's nature remains essentially unchanged, yet he should become more himself with each passing year.

I undertook great works; I built myself houses and planted vineyards; . . . I had possessions, more than any of my predecessors in Jerusalem; . . . I acquired all that man delights in. . . . Yes indeed, I got pleasure from all my labour. . . . Then I turned and reviewed all my handiwork, all my labour and toil, and I saw that everything was emptiness and chasing the wind, of no profit under the sun. . . . So I came to hate all my labour and toil here under the sun, since I should have to leave its fruits to my successor. . . . [So] I applied my mind to acquire wisdom (Eccl. 2:4,7,8,10,11,17; 8:16 NEB).

Solomon (the author of Ecclesiastes) was a good example of the consistency of one's motivational pattern. He had an experience of spiritual insight revealing that his acquisition of things was empty. Did his motivation then change? No. He acquired again, but now it was wisdom that was acquired. Similarly, because your pattern remains consistent, you will try to find some way to use it in every job or situation you are in. In spite of the sterility or the repressiveness of your environment, in spite of limited educational background, you will seek opportunity to somehow, some way exercise your motivational gifts. If you cannot use your pattern at work, you will find opportunity outside of work to use it. If you cannot use it at home, you will look elsewhere. If you cannot use it in school, you will seek satisfaction outside of school.

For example, we remember a successful manager in a large corporation telling us about his childhood. Jim was an only child on a Kansas farm. It was clear that his present position fit his managerial gifts, but we wondered what he would say about his childhood. How does an only child manage without brothers and sisters? How does a lonely boy on a remote farm find an outlet for his leadership gifts? Well, there may not have been people to manage, but there were chickens. It didn't take long for Jim to discover they could be managed, nor too much longer before Jim ended up with a chicken and egg business as a major boyhood achievement.

We also remember a ghetto child, with absolutely no encouragement from his fractured family and certainly none from his environment, who pursued his entrepreneurial interests. Rather than making money through questionable means, he had two businesses operating successfully before the age of twelve.

When it comes to motivated gifts, you will find a way!

Besides being permanent and consistent, your motivational pattern also controls your behavior. Consider this statement from the apostle Paul: "Even if I can preach the Gospel, I can claim no credit for it; I cannot help myself; it would be misery to me not to preach" (1 Cor. 9:16 NEB).

If you want response, you will seek out the unfilled needs people have. If you are an overcomer, you will seek a task no one has done before. If you are motivated to crusade, you will look for a cause. If you are motivated to function as a team member, you will look for a co-worker. If you are motivated to command, you will seek some way to get on top.

In other words, every job or role you occupy you will perceive and attempt to perform in accordance with your pattern of motivated behavior. What you emphasize, what you ignore, what you are lukewarm about—all reflect your pattern.

You and your pattern are one. You seek work and people and the church and theology and politics—and everything else in life of importance to you—through your motivational pattern, which is to say, your way of seeing and acting. You cannot act in just *any* way. You cannot perceive a situation from just *any* perspective. You can only act and perceive the way you act and perceive, which is so consistent and exact that it can be described in detail. Knowledge of that detail opens the way to true stewardship of your gifts. It makes you aware of what you want to do, releasing you from the idea that what you want to do and what ought to be done are necessarily the same.

This leads to our next consideration, the conflict between what our pattern insists we do and that which we ought to do. Sometimes, happily, those are the same, but often they are not. It is in this latter area that we discover character.

PART III
WORTHY OF THE VOCATION

7

Doing Your Thing
—Compulsively

IT IS GOOD TO KNOW THAT GOD MADE EACH OF us with a particular design that leads to generally consistent behavior. We do not awaken each day to be caught up into a chaos of unlimited possibilities for thinking, deciding, and acting, a bizarre universe in which anything could happen. We are able to engage in purposeful living. We have a capability for willfulness that enables us to shape our environment, that makes family life and civilization possible.

Each person carries out his God-given design in a very particular, consistent way that is truly individual. Each person cannot make decisions and be active in someone else's manner. Each functions in a unique style. Those are some of the things we have tried to establish so far.

Each style, however, is judged by others, who assign it a value. While it is possible to look at a motivational pattern being applied to a given situation and conclude that it is "consistent," a quality usually viewed as positive (we like people to be consistent) it is also possible to see the same motivational pattern being applied to another situation and conclude that it is "compulsive," a negative judgment.

For example, if you are in dire need of help, a person motivated to serve and help is going to be willing to do so and will likely be competent, and you will affirm the value of that gift. But the same individual who eagerly and repeatedly attempts to help when not needed will be seen as a compulsive "pain in the neck" by the victim of such insistence. Likewise, a person who is motivated to make a key contribution is seen as a savior or hero by those in need of that gift. But it is possible for those not requiring such a gift to see the same individual as a "person who must always have his say no matter what." One situation's consistent blessing is another's compulsive curse, according to each recipient's perspective.

It would seem that our value judgments in each of these cases are based objectively upon principles. In reality, however, they often are prompted by our needs or the values into which we have been initiated by our Christian subculture, rather than by biblical values. It is because motivated gifts functioning consistently can be the same as motivated gifts operating compulsively that the Scriptures are so dogmatic about the possibilities (specifically, the impossibility) of anyone's acting altruistically outside of the transforming power of Jesus Christ. We act the way we are motivated to act, whether the stage for such actions is criminal or humanitarian. In both cases, we play God by doing what we want to do, the way we want, when we want, regardless of what is needed or what others perceive as necessary.

Sometimes we can get away with it because our compulsion and the real need meet, or because we have a pattern that looks good to man's eyes. God, however, looks to our core and sees us doing what we intend out of a heart that is self-willed. It is not that motivated abilities are bad in and of themselves; after all, God designed them. It is that they are directed toward self-seeking, self-willed purposes.

Our self-centered determinations may be recognized by the world as success or as failure. They may benefit thousands of people or send us to prison. They may be considered enlightened intentions or clumsy and barbaric. Whatever judgments the world may make, however, they come from the world's understanding of what is good and bad. Such judgments may seem to have value. However, as Christians, we must remember that God judges out of holiness and so condemns all of it as unrighteous and of no profit. "None is righteous, no, not one" (Rom. 3:10 RSV). "Since all have sinned and fall short of the glory of God" (Rom. 3:23 RSV).

We are not permitted, from a biblical perspective, to divide an individual's nature into categories of bad and good. The totality of man's nature in its very essence is denounced as evil. The appearance of good behavior, lovely actions, and the gloss of civilization are categorically rejected by God along with the obvious evils of mankind. "Cursed is the man who trusts in man and makes flesh his arm, whose heart turns away from the LORD. . . . The heart is deceitful above all things, and desperately corrupt; who can understand it?" (Jer. 17:7,9 RSV).

The Scripture is so strong about this that some Christians proclaim the total depravity of man. Regardless of how far we go in our theological position, none of us comprehends the depths of man's sin. The one whose heart departs from God does not always appear in the guise of blatant evil. He appears as my neighbor. Worse, he appears as me.

God wants you to be free to choose to do what you are gifted to do *when* He wants you to do it. This is a crucial point to understand. It means there are times when you are expected to deny yourself by not exercising your abilities, even if a situation calls for it. It means that you are given the power to do what God knows and wills ought to be done, regardless of what you want to do. For example, you may know what your troubled friend should do, but you sit on your gift because you realize your friend is open to someone else's counsel at that moment.

The only way we know to enter into that liberty is to go through a "making holy" process called sanctification, which we will discuss in the next chapter. It cannot be attained merely through self-discipline. You may have success withholding a move you are motivated to make, but remember that basic to Christianity is the fact that man cannot save himself through self-sacrifice or self-denial.

God is not pleased with half-way measures. He always moves perfectly, which is to say, He moves all the way. Where we may judge a disciplined approach to a situation as being good, He is looking for the best. He wants you not only to withhold the exercise of your gifts when you should not use them, but He also wants you to enjoy being in that position. Isn't that a paradox!

Did God design you a certain way and then expect you to be able to enjoy denying the way He made you? Not exactly. God as the designer not only has the detail of your design in mind, but also all the designs of all people in their interrelated complexity. He intended a variety of interdependent designs. In the church, the ministry of each person complements the ministry of another. In society, each individual has a different role and differing jobs. God has His eye on the whole fabric, as well as on each thread.

Because of our fallen natures, we think about our patterns in isolation and live in a world that is unable to perceive and obey the overall design God intended for humanity as a whole. We act as if our purposes were to fulfill ourselves, when in reality we are to fulfill God's grand, overall design. God's intention produces the harmonious effect of having each individual fulfilled while fulfilling others.

Therefore, regardless of the temporary joy of applause or financial return, an isolated exercise of your motivated abilities (where you decide everything) is dangerous. It is a small, duplicate version of Lucifer's deciding that his understanding was better than God's. This attitude that is ours through the disobedient race that fathered us seems natural, and it works its distortion even after conversion. However, as Christians we can camouflage our stubborn, self-willed intentions. We can mask our willfulness with the whitewash of spiritual principles.

For example, in Bible study class you might insist on a certain interpretation of Scripture that requires people to meet specific behavior standards as defined by you. Then we discover your motivational thrust is *meeting needs and fulfilling requirements*. Your gift will give that scriptural emphasis authority, but it may be your, not God's, authority. There is no doubt how *you* will see things. At issue here is your willingness to pray for the understanding of what God intends for the Bible class.

Another example is the person who is always pressing his

subordinates to meet ever higher production quotas as a principle of good work, but whose motivational thrust, we discover,
is to *meet the challenge*. There are right times and wrong times
for that emphasis. We cannot expect a person with that primary
motivation to tell the difference on his own, or to easily see
another perspective by himself.

The person motivated to function independently is likely to
strike out against his boss or a controlling-type committee
chairman. He is apt to be skilled in discovering anyone's Achil-
les heel. In contrast to this person, another individual motivated
to follow may look like a saint because he is standing against the
independent brother by affirming the leader. In essence, they
are both being prompted by the compulsiveness of their motivation.

It is not that any of those motivations are bad in and of
themselves. Bad is exercising a gift compulsively. It means
centering so strongly upon what is wanted that it cuts off God's
will and guidance. The result is a gift that is not free to function
according to His plan but is compelled to function independently. This is so important to understand that we will devote
the rest of the chapter to examples from the list of central
motivational thrusts described on pages 68 and 69.

Keep in mind as you read the examples that everyone is
unique, that no one fits exactly and completely into any category, and that we are speaking in generalities. Given all that,
however, you might be surprised at how similar you are to
others with the same central motivational thrust.

If you are motivated to *acquire-possess*, you will be a great
source of wisdom for your partners in business expansion,
evaluating financial strategies, and making other sound business decisions. However, you also will be very possessive of
your belongings at home and will not easily lend your
lawnmower to neighbors. You will become anxious if you
cannot have complete control over your own work project. You
can get "hot under the collar" if the missionary committee
wants to overspend, yet favor the church's building an extension. You would take a very dim view of selling your home to

move into a communal living situation. You might move to a church with substantial physical facilities, but you would not be likely to accept theology supporting a "sell what you have and give to the poor" movement.

If you are motivated to *be in charge-command*, people will naturally turn to you at work in times of indecision and need for strong leadership. Somehow you will always end up in charge of every new product development committee, the PTA, your bowling league. When not in charge, you will probably criticize the plans or actions of the leadership. You will spend an inordinate amount of time at work, at home, at the every member canvass, to make sure things are run right. You will get very anxious about programs being managed by a committee. You will move to a church favoring strong lay leadership. You will embrace a theology promoting hierarchical relationships in the church, family, and at work.

If you are motivated to *combat-prevail*, much of the church will rally round your call to arms when national leadership begins to flirt with overly liberal positions. At work, your company assigns you customers who are being wooed by competitors. However, you also will get into wrestling matches with people who have strong opinions in your building committee, your Bible study group, and your computer evaluation task force. You will come near to killing yourself with long hours spent organizing opposition to a proposed relocation of your department, a plan to remove the pastor, or a threatened commercial development of the town park. You will favor a church engaged in a lot of social action and a theology of attacking and conquering evil forces in society.

If you are motivated to *excel-be the best*, you will have made major contributions to the vigor and growth of your sales territory. However, you also will work yourself to a frazzle in the new member canvass, beating all previous records. You will urge your church to give more to missions than any other church in your part of the country. You will urge your kids to get A's, make the varsity, get the lead role. You will urge your boss to replace the old computer in favor of the fastest one available.

You will move to a church and a denomination that are considered the best in your area, and you will favor a theology in which God is seen to reward the fruitful servant.

If you are motivated to *gain a response-influence*, clients will extol your warmth and personality as a customer service representative, and you will be known for your personal record of evangelism. You will spend excessive time preparing a presentation that will dazzle the program committee with your plans, or trying to find an eloquent speaker, or creating magnificent decorations and ingenious games. You will spend twelve hours practicing a half-hour talk for an adult Sunday school class. You will carefully politic each member of the school board before the vote on the busing program. You will move to a church spending one-third of its budget on missionary work. You might favor a theology of prayer in which God can be moved by the penitent.

If you are motivated to *gain recognition-attention*, you may have been an elder and lay leader for the maximum number of terms allowed and may be well-known throughout your company for your past contributions. You will likely play other visible roles: choir, Scripture reading, public prayers, giving testimonials, or missionary work. You will favor a company newspaper and items in the Sunday worship program publicizing activities and the people responsible. You will bring any project you work on to a conclusion that can be reported on and formally noticed by others. You will favor a church in a "good" location that builds up its lay people. You will be attracted to a theology emphasizing personal salvation and might be less enthusiastic for teachings about humility.

If you are motivated to *make the team-grade*, you have probably been promoted at work recently and are generally known as very dependable and "a real comer." You will tend to climb the ladder of church success, first as a worker, then as a committee head, and finally as a deacon or elder. You will probably join the country club, rank high in a service organization, and end up being a member of an elite group in your church, work, or community. You probably remained in an

Army reserve unit and received promotions since your active service days. You may be overly literal in your personal devotional life, disciplined in reading the literature and following the regimen prescribed by the next level up. You'll probably join a church with a hierarchical structure, and you will favor a theology having clear standards of conduct.

If you are motivated to *exploit-achieve potential*, you will be known at work as the change agent, the idea person. However, you'll probably also encourage the assistant minister who shouldn't have been hired. You might urge the fundraising committee to use pressure tactics. You might recommend use of the pastor's home for an expanded Sunday school without first asking for his permission. You will promote the use of mainly high-achieving young people to lead more of the services. You might be attracted to an emerging church. You would probably favor a theology encouraging personal growth and development.

If you are motivated to *meet needs-fulfill expectations*, you're probably known at work as the person to go to when you want something done. You're likely to spend much time responding to problem situations at work and in your community involving widows, kids in trouble, failing marriages, and families with sick breadwinners. However, you're also likely to rise to any request made by the pastor for your services; in fact, you find it difficult to refuse anybody who comes to you with a need, a problem, or an expectation. You will join a church active in charitable projects, and you will favor a theology in which the requirements for growth and spiritual "success" are well-defined.

If you are motivated to *make work-make effective*, you're probably known at work as "Mr. Turn-Around" who has resurrected several problem departments. You will focus on people or machines that do not work, programs that cannot get off the ground. You will spend every Saturday morning for six months getting the church bookstore on a sound basis and functioning properly. You'll probably oppose replacing the church heating system that keeps breaking down. You'd join a church that is operating on three cylinders. You'd favor a theology teaching the possibility that mankind can harmoniously work together.

If you are motivated to *master-perfect*, your place of work may be impeccably neat and efficient. You may be responsible for your church's lending tape library, which rivals a professional studio in its completeness. However, you will hang in on the details of a discussion after everyone else wants to go home. You will throw cold water on any scheme not well-thought-out. You will back away from any activity or responsibility you cannot adequately control or prepare for. You will favor a church where things are done decently and in order.

If you are motivated to *overcome-persevere*, you are the one chosen by your company when it has a mountain to climb. However, you will start a school without any in-depth planning or financial support. You will drive all night in a blizzard to keep an appointment. You will take on the zoning board over your right to raise pigs on the church property. You reject everyone's advice and enter seminary at age forty-four. You will seek a church attempting to integrate for the first time, or that is meeting over a delicatessen, and you will favor a theology that requires the believer to bleed before he is saved, emphasizing works.

There are many more motivational examples than we can describe here. These are characterizations and therefore somewhat exaggerated. In actuality, they would vary quite a bit in detail from individual to individual. But they are helpful in seeing how our own motivations tend to move us. Our work, our life at home and in the church often are shaped by our motivated desires when we should seek to recognize actual needs. The church does not exist merely to give us an opportunity to do what we want. Our theological leanings ought to issue more from scriptural convictions and less from personal inclination.

The Scriptures need to be the norm for Christian life and belief, not one's motivations. That is why listening to the Holy Spirit teach and confirm the truths of Scripture is of paramount importance in order to read what the Word is actually saying and not what we want it to say. We should submit to God's orchestration of the gifts in the church and the scriptural disciplines that intend the good of the whole as well as the good of the individual.

Years of working with people's motivated abilities have convinced us of the importance of this. We see no possibility in perceiving the norms God has for us outside Scripture, but Scripture as it is, not exploited to justify our independent ideas. One's gifts will naturally create a variety in emphasis, a condition that adds interest, but they should never introduce confusion.

Two other correctives are also available. One is found in the sanctifying process the Holy Spirit leads us through that in some ways never ends in our lifetime. The other is in the balance possible in the complementary use of gifts available in the fellowship of other Christians. We will deal with the sanctifying process in the next chapters, and subsequently with Christian fellowship.

8

Playing God

WITH ALL THE EXAMPLES OF THE LAST CHAP-
ter, it should not be difficult to review your own personal history
and discover where you operated compulsively to get what you
wanted. It is the common lot of the human race to repeatedly
pursue one's own personal vision, goals, projects, or relationships, preoccupied with an insistence on getting one's own way.
Each of us knows what is best, in spite of the diversity of
opinions or possibilities that exist in a given situation.

What are we doing when we insist on getting our way, when
we use our God-given, motivated patterns for selfish interests?
Our answer is that we are playing God. We not only want to do
what we want how and when we want, but we also want our
desires to have priority over everyone else's. To have one's
intentions honored before all others is a matter of divine pre-
rogative. We are competing with God, a contest we are sure to
lose, but one we take on nevertheless.

Why are we so compulsive about playing God? It is in our
blood. When Adam and Eve decided that their understanding,
their perception of reality, should have priority over Jehovah's,
they acquired a disease that has become a congenital plague for
mankind. Rationality, education, self-discipline, culture, science, psychology, and law have not healed the disease of sin
and cannot heal it. There is no power in man to heal himself,
which is why Scripture describes mankind as totally helpless in
the situation. Only Jesus Christ provides a cure. ''For as by one
man's disobedience many were made sinners, so by one man's
obedience many will be made righteous'' (Rom. 5:19 RSV).

When we attempt to play God, we do so with some knowledge of what is involved. Because we are made in His image, we have an inherent sense of what qualities reside in such a role, and we can display fanatical preoccupation with them.

One such preoccupation is the intense desire to be blameless. We want our appearance to be faultless. We want our work to be above criticism. We justify ourselves in all our actions. We are defensive about our mistakes. We have excuses for our failures. We hide our faults.

Not only do we want to be above reproach, but we also want to be better than others. We want to get the credit. In comparison with others, we want to be recognized as possessing more quality, more material things, a better personality, and greater beauty in spite of any evidence to the contrary. Using whatever standards are in fashion, we want to be placed above the common man.

This is not to be confused with those whose gift involves comparison with others, those who are genuinely unique or who love healthy competition or advancement. We are referring to the lust in us to be above all others, the self-centeredness in all mankind.

Third, as already mentioned, we want our will to be supreme. What we believe to be most important we insist is just that. We also assume our priorities to be right, our perspective to be correct, our perceptions to be accurate. Therefore, what we want done in any situation is precisely what we believe ought to be done.

Those symptoms of wanting to be God are obvious in some people and hidden in others. Adolf Hitler and Joseph Stalin may have usurped power on a scale that most of us are denied, and the magnitude of their crimes may be in large contrast to what we intend in life. But behind the mask of many a gracious person hides a dictator in whose hands equal opportunity for power would produce precious little difference in performance. Behind all our facades is the man who would be king.

What does God say about this? What is His opinion? Fire upon Sodom and Gomorrah, floods upon the earth, and plagues upon Egypt are graphic examples of divine attitude. So also is death upon a cross, and it is that particular judgment with which the Christian identifies. There is his hope—that the dictator in his heart can be judged as evil, nailed to the cross, and executed to trouble him no more. The apostle Paul's title for the dictator is the "old self," which is to be put to death in us so as to save us from his insatiable demands. "We know that our old self was crucified with him so that the sinful body might be destroyed, and we might no longer be enslaved to sin" (Rom. 6:6 rsv).

The Will

The "dictator" within us does not take casual residence in one of the outer chambers of our being. He seeks to control the center of communications and the seat of power. He dwells in the will. There he influences our relationships and impinges upon the nature and effectiveness of our work. The will controls our being through its causative power. The stuff of which it is made is intention and motivation. Thoughts and actions cannot begin without the primary, initiating power of the will, the heart of our being. That is why King Solomon warned us in Scripture to "keep your heart with all vigilance; for from it flow the springs of life" (Prov. 4:23 rsv). Jeremiah, as the spokesman for God, wrote: "I the LORD search the mind and try the heart, to give to every man according to his ways,* according to the fruit of his doings" (Jer. 17:10 rsv).

In the gospel stories of Christ's ministry, we can see that He was not preoccupied with the symptoms of sin, though He healed them. Rather, he was intent on the cause, which is to say that He focused on what individuals willed in their lives. He looked to their hearts. "Which is easier, to say, 'Your sins are forgiven you,' or to say, 'Rise and walk'?" (Luke 5:23 rsv).

The attitude of one's heart is increasingly the starting point for effective healing of the body, the emotions, or the intellect.

---

* Otherwise defined from the Hebrew as meaning "mode of action," about as close to the word *motivation* as you can get (*Strong's Exhaustive Concordance*).

The first question in each of these cases should probably be, "Do you want to be well?" The medical field has recognized that people who have a strong will to live are more likely to survive than those whose willful hold on life is weak. In personal counseling, too, the attitude of the will is central. There are those who spend a long time in therapy because there is no recognition by either the counselor or the subject that there is no intention to get well. We are astounded at the number of people whose identities are tied to their sickness or who fear the responsibilities that would be theirs if they became healthy. People can become so familiar with ill health that being well seems abnormal to them. They are secure in sickness, and the script of their lives can easily be compared to a television soap opera. Trouble seems to give meaning to life.

What is true about physical and emotional health is also true about intellectual health. There are intelligent people who will believe strange things. It is not necessarily weakness of mind or irrationality that compels them. Often people believe what they want to believe, even when they recognize untruth in what they believe. That is especially perverse, because one of the major functions of the mind is to identify error.

As an example, one of us can tell a story that took place several years ago. I had a visit from a student I had not seen in several years. He was eager to argue for a Western hybrid of an Eastern religion he had embraced. After we had exchanged news about each other, it didn't take long before we were immersed in the heat of discussion. I fully expected to win the argument by leading him step by logical step into a corner, but in the middle of this verbal chess game, I believe I was prompted by the Holy Spirit to recognize my motive and question his. In my case, I realized that my primary goal was simply to win the argument. I was exploiting Truth to come out on top. Swift repentance was the corrective.

For the student's sake, I found myself asking, "Before we go any further, may I ask a question? Are you willing, whatever turns out to be true, to believe what is true regardless of whether it is you, me, or someone else who is proved right?"

I cannot remember if I had to repeat such a convoluted question, but I do remember the strange silence as he pondered his answer. Expecting a quick and logical "Of course," I was surprised as the excitement on his face faded and he painfully sought the truth. I waited for the answer to what I could see had become a disturbing question. His response was obviously honest but strangely brutal as he dropped a quiet "No" into the silence. I was shocked as we simultaneously realized that he was willing to believe what he knew to be a lie.

That one incident has forced us to avoid propaganda carefully in presenting the gospel and to look for God's timing in any strategy of apologetics. We cannot assume that people always want to be reasonable or that they will yield to truth if we present it with authority and clarity. The father of lies does bring deception, but worse, there are times when *we* choose to believe a lie. The will tends to bend the intelligence to its own desire, cutting off access to truth.

Because the will is the key to the mental, physical, and spiritual health of every individual, Jesus Christ calls us to have our intentions converted. Jesus insists on repentance, that we invite Him into the center of our beings to set us free from the dictatorial rule of the "old self," that we put on a new man, free to be obedient to God's will. God wants to be the object of our wills, the one on whom our hearts are set.

The Shape of the Will

The words *to be willing* are often interchangeable with the words *to be motivated,* so when we write about motivated abilities, we are suggesting that they emerge from the core of one's being. They emerge from the will.

To know the pattern of an individual's motivated abilities is like knowing the shape of that person's will. That is why they were described in chapter 6 as being permanent, consistent, and controlling. We know, now, that motivated gifts are intimately part of our nature, that when we are willful, we are willful in a very particular way. We do not want to do just anything. We only want to do certain things, and we do them the way we are motivated to do them, even when we are playing God.

When God deals with our idolatry, He cannot exclude motivated abilities, for they are one of the major ways we carry out our self-centered intentions. He must deal with them in a radical way. He has His method; Christians often have theirs.

Some "Christian" Methods

Christians are offered all kinds of techniques promising the possibility of arriving at spiritual maturity by going through a disciplined process or program of teaching or submission to certain rules. Often they are devised and taught by Christian leaders who do not realize that they may be imposing or proposing a system that comes out of their own motivational pattern, or out of their enthusiasm for a system of discipline that was successful in their own lives. For example:

- A leader who is motivated to control is prone to devise a "death to self" community in which participants give up their "willfulness" to satisfy his.
- A Christian leader who is motivated to build relations with others is likely to support a one-on-one discipleship program.
- A person motivated to persevere is not necessarily going to be disciplined by tough prayer vigils and fasting.
- A Christian who is motivated to gain recognition might be attracted to the charismatic movement, not necessarily because of theological convictions, but because of the opportunities it might provide for visibility.

The kinds of techniques that are embraced for the sake of spiritual discipline need to be individual. A set of rules made to discipline a person who has one motivational pattern may actually encourage unsanctified expression of another's pattern.

Scripture does not outline one specific, step-by-step program aimed at maturing all Christians. Each individual requires a unique strategy. What one person needs will not work for another. What cripples one Christian may be a sign of health in another. This is troubling to those who want Christians in a more standardized package. God, however, has made each of us unique and never tires of ministering to every need.

Whatever method He uses in each life, God requires us to put aside our silly attempts to be god. Where we pretend to be blameless, He would have us confess our sin and receive the gift of Christ's righteousness. Where we want to be better than all others, He would have us be humble and eager for others to be praised. Where we want to get our way, He would have us follow His way. Where we would attempt to replace bad behavior with good, He would replace both with holiness. Many years of teaching our emotions and intellects wrong attitudes, many years of gathering subconscious distortions and self-congratulatory intentions, and many self-deceptive motives and illusions need to be repented of and changed.

God's Method

God's goal in interfering with our lives to bring about such change is very simple: He wants us to discover our real identities. The method God uses to change us is called sanctification, and though there are theological disagreements about how it is brought about, we can consider the essentials and define sanctification as "being made holy." Holiness is an essential characteristic of God's personality. As we stated earlier, God does not choose between good and evil. He consists of good to such an infinite degree that the word *holy* was invented to express such awesome righteousness.

In order to be compatible with His nature when we come into relationship with God, we must become holy. "Be holy, for I am holy" (Lev. 11:44 RSV). There are two ways of looking at the sanctifying process, and both are necessary to the Christian life.

Holiness as a gift

The instant we repent of our sin and are converted, we immediately come into right relationship with God. As new members of the Body of Christ, we receive the love of Christ that sanctifies us and makes us clean (see Eph. 5:26). Note Paul's use of past-tense verbs in these two verses: "God chose you from the beginning to be saved, through sanctification by the Spirit and belief in the truth" (2 Thess. 2:13 RSV). "You were washed, you were sanctified, you were justified in the name of the Lord Jesus Christ" (1 Cor. 6:11 RSV). Sanctification is thus already accomplished, a status to be enjoyed by the Christian.

Sanctification as a process

But holiness also needs to be worked out in our lives, so in another sense, sanctification is a process requiring discipline and vigorous Christian living.

Work out your own salvation with fear and trembling; for God is at work in you, both to will and to work for his good pleasure (Phil. 2:12, 13 RSV).

And have you forgotten the exhortation which addresses you as sons?—"My son, do not regard lightly the discipline of the Lord, nor lose courage when you are punished by him. For the Lord disciplines him whom he loves, and chastises every son whom he receives" (Heb. 12:5, 6 RSV).

Since we have these promises, beloved, let us cleanse ourselves from every defilement of body and spirit, and make holiness perfect in the fear of God (2 Cor. 7:1 RSV).

"Completing our consecration" is a good description of the sanctification process, because it recognizes a consecration that has already taken place while also recognizing that our lives must still be conformed to the example of Christ our Lord.

Maintaining the Balance

There is a need to keep this dual view of sanctification in balance. If we only concentrate on the fact of our holy standing in Christ, the finished work, we receive the joy of being blameless and free before God while ignoring our susceptibility to temptation, not to say successful temptation. The arrival of the latter then destroys our confidence in the reality of our salvation.

If we emphasize standards of behavior, on the other hand, we may enjoy the evidence of self-discipline but end up with legalism, with its crippling guilt, when we make a slip.

The balanced view says that because of God's actions, we *now* possess our salvation. We express it, however, by cleansing every defilement from our body and spirit, by making holiness perfect in the fear of God (2 Cor. 7:1). In short, we are given the choice to confirm our sanctification in Christ by corresponding behavior.

This is a matter of a good deal of confusion for many Christians. An almost schizophrenic approach has confounded believers everywhere as they listen to the preaching of salvation by grace while submitting to the imposition of a Christian lifestyle that is in reality submission to the laws of Christian behavior. We are not interested in teaching that you ought to be set free by Christ from the compulsiveness of your motivations, only to embrace slavery to rules of disciplines to keep those motivations in their place. Rather, we believe that God works from the inside out.

Starting from the outside with right behavior (even if it is "Christian" behavior) and expecting it to change inward nature is not God's way. It does not bring salvation—grace does (Eph. 2:8). That grace is in us in the person of Jesus Christ—*now* within us, radically affecting the source of all behavior (our wills). As He takes over more levels of our interior beings, conforming our wills to His, new behavior patterns will increasingly replace the old behavior patterns. This process will continue to increase, though perhaps not as neatly or as swiftly as we would prefer, and at varying rates in different individuals.

Confining our concerns, as is usually done, to moral and lifestyle behavior patterns falls short of an overall appreciation of creation. Behavior at home, work, and play is included in God's grace. So is how we behave intellectually, imaginatively, emotionally, and motivationally.

To develop an understanding of how the motivational patterns are sanctified, it first must be recognized that though God is the source of the pattern, and, therefore, it is a gift and a blessing, it also is always a potential curse, because of sin. A person's individual pattern is his major medium for expressing self-centeredness, and it is at the same time the means by which he can express conformation to God's will as already designed into his nature.

We are aware that there are extreme teachings about sanctification that have recurred in the history of the church and are still with us. For instance, man's gifts are sometimes pictured as worthless. We quote some Christians: "Don't thank me. It wasn't me who did it, it was the Lord." "In myself, I can't love you. I am just a pipeline of God's love to you." "My will must die, and God's will must take over." We do not want to minimize the importance of humility. But it ought not to be overemphasized at the expense of God's glory. God is not honored by our pretending that His creative powers are less than they really are. God did not create robots or marionettes. Divine genius created man with an enormous capacity to will and to do.

Obedience is a key to understanding this aspect of our relationship to God. Robots cannot be obedient; they can only be programmed. Human beings are the ones who can be obedient. And obedience is not Jesus Christ coming into our lives and gradually replacing our wills with His, taking over each area of our beings until He is supreme dictator—a kind of divine fascism. Obedience requires two wills, God's will and our will. But our wills must increasingly exercise their freedom of choice in the direction of obedience to His will. The more vigorous our wills are in acknowledging the rightness of and deferring to His, the purer the obedience.

9

Becoming That New Creation in Christ

IN MOST LIVES WE HAVE STUDIED, OF THOSE who have submitted to the process of sanctification, the early months and years after conversion are spent experiencing a variety of spiritual confrontations that are a part of change and growth.

Natural Changes

There are changes that seemingly require no decisions but that spring out of you naturally because of obedience to the call of Jesus. A new love for others and a change in your vocabulary are only two common examples. There seems to be a spontaneous response to the presence of Jesus Christ within you. The response in some people may look much like the actions of a lovesick schoolboy. In others, we see the sober actions of someone who knows a new presence in his life. In either case, a different inner attitude and sometimes a sharply different behavioral style emerge as natural expressions of new life.

Disciplined Changes

Other changes are less spontaneous and come out of obedient decisions you make as you perceive issues with which the Holy Spirit is asking you to deal. You find a growing awareness that you no longer march to the orders of the enemy of your soul, but that you are a prince or princess of the King of Kings and that you should order your life accordingly. Here are a few examples:

Excesses

If your motivations include certain kinds of influencing abilities and you enjoy being with people in social situations, you may be asked to examine your excesses of drinking, smoking, and partying. Others, more private in their motivational pursuits, may want to think twice about watching television thirty hours a week, reading five books, or working late four nights a week. They are being freed from the prisons they created for themselves, whatever and wherever they exist.

Habit

If your motivations include a rigid system of personal rewards or an insistence on always leading your life the way you want, you may be asked to stop doing those things that you "have" to do to be happy or satisfied—for example, the Sunday and Monday football game, a cup of coffee at 10:15 A.M., dinner at 5:30 P.M., Wednesday night out, every other morning jog, Sunday morning golf round, or sacred times alone. You are being shaken free from your idols and teddy bears.

Relationships

If you are strong at opening people up to your advice and counsel, you may have to cut out the incessant coffee hours and people calling or dropping in day and night to get some help on a problem. You are being reoriented and helped to see how compulsive you are and how you make others dependent on you. (Do not fret, you will have all the relationships you could ever desire.)

Imaginations

If you are motivationally imaginative or otherwise have a hyperactive thought life, you may be asked to give up thought patterns that consume your time, particularly if they tend to be mired in a sailor-on-leave mentality. These would include not only sexual fantasies, but also the hurts you have suffered or your scheming, your preoccupation with the personal or material or status possessions of others, and dreams of grandeur and glory and what might have been. Unhealthy ambition also fits in this category.

Irritations

If you are motivated to get results or get ahead, you may have bad attitudes about certain associates, telephone operators, people you think are stupid, situations you cannot stand, people you cannot stand, people who cross you, people who want to control you, being asked to do things beneath you, or trivia that prevents you from doing what you want to do. Many of those irritations need to undergo examination, and you will be asked to release some, especially in view of God's love for you and what He has forgiven you for doing and being.

Facades and faces

God cannot abide pretense and phoniness. Many people motivated to influence others or to play certain roles have different faces they put on to meet different people and situations. Whether you smile all the time, you pride yourself on being an "up front" person under all circumstances, you are a chameleon, you are a saint in public and have no time for your family, you are a politician at the office and a tyrant with your kids, or you are a saint on Sunday and a Scrooge on Monday —God will reveal your pretense so you can decide to do otherwise.

While the above should be some of the expected behavioral objectives for you as a Christian, it seems unwise to use them or any like them as standards to measure whether anybody else is a Christian. There are non-Christians who can produce similar behavior patterns. In fact, there are non-Christian religions that often produce better behavior.

Inner Changes

There are items in the above list that cannot be put aside through decision-making. Try as you might, you may discover that you have besetting sins that continue to plague you even after conversion. This is especially difficult to deal with if there is clear evidence of outstanding change in other areas of your life where controlling habits that troubled you for years suddenly were removed without any effort on your part. Many ex-alcoholics or ex-drug users can testify to the reality of such swift changes.

Please remember that what the Bible calls besetting sins are not evidence of a partial conversion experience. Either we are Christians or we are not, spiritually alive or spiritually dead. It is true that some new births are vigorous, others less so. That indicates degrees of vitality that affect the quality of Christian living, but the matter of whether a person is or is not Christian is quite settled and not dependent on one's current level of spiritual maturity.

For many, besetting sins can be overcome by increased spiritual strength, by bringing listless Christian living up to greater vigor through proper spiritual diet and exercise. But for those who have a healthy, vital spiritual lifestyle and still are troubled by actions, fears, or other responses that are discordant, there is a need to rest on the previously mentioned fact that God works from the inside out. It is not good strategy in this kind of situation to try to reverse the divine process by imposing the rigor of self-discipline upon the symptoms. That creates the hot and cold experiences of emotional highs during stretches of success and despairing lows in times of failure, with their accompanying doubts about the reality of being a child of God.

You are a Christian through a covenant agreement that continues in spite of your feelings. When a person is married, he is bound by a contractual agreement that is a fact whether he looks married or not, whether he feels married or not. Similarly, your covenant relationship with God is quite fixed. Our grief over seemingly uncontrollable patterns of feeling or behavior may be evidence that our relationship to God is effective, else we would not care so much.

Some of these deeply rooted qualities may be in your motivated behavior. Some people have a great fear of rejection if building relationships is motivationally crucial to them. Others have special anxiety about investments they have made if making money is of critical importance to them. People who are motivationally strong at controlling situations and other people can develop an incredible array of compulsive techniques and ploys to always have their way, as well as a deep hostility toward what might remove that power. For a variety of motivational reasons, people are inclined to trust themselves to get done what they want done and not trust God to bless them, so all sorts of habits and fixations get encrusted in the soul.

Other difficult-to-change behavior patterns are psychological or emotional in nature. Our psychologically oriented society has a rich vocabulary to contribute here: phobia, neurosis, compulsion, nervous disorder, trauma, and aberrant behavior. Whatever the word, such people react or behave in ways that in no way can be considered healthy. These are situations requiring skilled counseling, and if you think you are in need of such, we encourage you to find a counselor who combines professional gifts with the spiritual gifts of discernment and wisdom. Remember these familiar verses: "Come to me, all who labor and are heavy-laden, and I will give you rest. Take my yoke upon you, and learn from me; for I am gentle and lowly in heart and you will find rest for your souls. For my yoke is easy, and my burden is light" (Matt. 11:28–30 RSV).

Do not be surprised by your defeats, but expect victory from God. Move away from endless self-evaluations of your failures to the position where you hold God responsible for success, since ultimately He is the *only* source. "The secret is this: Christ in you, the hope of a glory to come" (Col. 1:27 NEB). This Scripture pictures an enormous personal force within us that is certain to move everything connected with it to the state of glory. Open the closed chambers of your heart to Him for refurbishing and restoration. Relate those places to the Christ within you, and you will discover beauty as He is allowed to move into each floor of your interior house and take it over, room by room.

While most Christians point with delight to the easy successes that come at the point of conversion, most do not speak of the secret battle that continues in one area or another after conversion. It seems to be a fact of Christian maturity that we are involved with interior wars of no small consequence. Those who are not, we suspect, have allowed self-ignorance to blunt their growth or are too anemic to enjoin conflict. The fiercer battles take place in those who have been exposed to a long history of successful enemy operations within. Such a history of inner devastations requires a process of constructive reversal on the part of Christ in us.

There seems to be a common element to those types of problems in that they are almost always rooted in our self-integrity, the wholeness of our self-identity and worth. The sins of fear are related to the insecurity of self. Sexual sins and sexual distortions are often evidence of a damaged self-nature. So are feelings of inferiority, which are evidence of lies in the way one assesses self-worth.

God works steadily in our innermost beings with those kinds of sins, because they are not easily shed. They have to do with our core and require internal changes in us if they are to be removed. God does not violate the inner territories of our personalities. The will must be exercised, giving permission for change and being changed itself while doing so.

We can discover that God is our ultimate security and relive the times when such awareness was not possible, thereby fusing truth into those old memories, changing their effect on the present. We can discover the sexual model God has for us and thereby bring integrity into our nature and its expression to others. Inferiority can be gradually overcome as we locate and embrace the good gifts within us and commune with the loving giver of those gifts. What others wrote on our price tag can be replaced by what Christ actually paid for us.

Quick answers are a vain hope for problems that involve the stuff of which our personalities are made. We must acquiesce to the process of development, knowing that it takes time. But we do so hopefully, with the knowledge of God's eagerness for us to become the uniquely and fully developed men and women He created us to be.

Changes in Our Work

The Christian serious about union with Christ can expect anything that negatively affects the quality of spiritual fruit produced in his life to be given some divine attention. Whether you run a business, a machine tool, or a grease rack; whether you are called mommy, doctor, or hey you; whether you farm or argue for a living, sell or buy, assemble or maintain, in the front line or at headquarters—all that makes little difference. You are to produce good fruit that is pleasing to God.

Perhaps you work at one tiny specialty in one large function of one huge organization. If you are well-placed where you are, there is a way to perform that job that is worthy of praise, and your functioning that way is important to you and to God. Peruse a book on the physiology of some specific organ or sand worm and tell us God is not concerned with details or what goes on in department AU-792. Do you think God does not care about a clean base hit, sparkling water, light but clinging spaghetti sauce, clothing that enhances who you are, sperm whales, efficient combustion engineering, healthy tomatoes, orderly files, stimulating lectures on economics, loving discipline, durable shock absorbers, picking up garbage noiselessly? None of it is remotely possible without Him.

Do you think the One who has embraced agony for you is unconcerned about the sloppy, undisciplined way you might be proceeding with the ten talents He gave you to invest? Look at each of the following common problem areas that are tied in with your motivated behavior. See if any require your attention.

Craftsmanship

Where your foundation of knowledge is shallow (because you are motivated to learn just to secure some immediate goal); your quality is a little shoddy (because you are only motivated to meet the standards set by your peers); your predilection is to take questionable shortcuts (because you want only to finish and go home); your touch is a trifle rusty (because you have concentrated too much on promotion); your thoroughness is often nonexistent (because you are motivated to get on to the next project); or your openness to new technology is somewhat dubious (because you love being the expert and you already know the old technology)—you may start getting inner nudges (or a sharp rap) to improve your scholarship, stop a bad practice, fill a void in your arsenal, or spend more time doing something no one else sees, even though the payoff is obscure. God is the Master Craftsman and would have your workmanship be beyond question.

Relationships

If you only have time for people who can do something for you (because you are motivated to exploit potential); if you find you have a tendency to put others down (because you are motivated to be in charge); if you find large areas of your life, thinking, and feeling closed to outsiders (because of your supersensitivity to appearances and impressions); if you have a hardness of heart about certain people you work with (because they won't be influenced by your gift of persuasion); if all you know about your associates is their work life (because you are totally absorbed by your job); if you do not care enough about people who work for you to get involved with them (because you are afraid of your inability to keep impressing them); if you only see others as souls to be saved and not people who are His creation (because you are numbers- and results-oriented)—God may start opening you up to new relationships, melting down your hardness, opening your eyes to needs you can fulfill. God is the author of love and would have you as a vessel for giving His love to others, so He needs to use your gifts (His gifts, actually), but can't until you focus on Him and not on yourself.

Stress and strain

As a Christian, your heart is not to be tied up with man's approval. You want to serve your fellow man well, but you do not work to please man, but rather God. Any tendency to go up or down on the basis of today's strokes, any coming apart at the seams because ''important'' people are looking you over, any agony over the possibility of termination, is probably evidence that your treasures are in the gold market, not on eternal fruit. God wants to help you live in the world but not be enslaved by its systems.

How you respond to stress is a witness. How you handle disappointment is a witness. How you take criticism and rebuke —fair and unfair—speaks more than a hundred testimonies.

The gray zone

If you tend to live in partial truths, make promises you cannot keep, betray confidences, give false impressions, speak words that hurt, curse, undermine, or attract the wrong kind of attention, God would purify with truth and would convict you of the sin in your heart and tongue.

Giving up our teddy bears and the "little pleasures" of life, facing our neuroses and acts of selfishness and arrogance, doing what is psychologically excruciating, is not what many of us want to face. As a matter of fact, if there is any way out, most of us will avoid dealing with those problems, at least the more serious of them.

The above kinds of "minor" sins (in man's eyes, not God's) prevent us from being who we should be. They also disturb the lives of others. In addition, they deny Christ the fragrance of gifts well-invested and used, and that cannot possibly be a small matter.

A word about expectations of others

Be careful that the principles you discover in the spiritual successes that come your way do not become your measuring stick for others. Recognize motivational differences. What you can handle with gracious aplomb may be infuriating to another because of his motivations. However, you might be provoked into conduct unbecoming a trapped lion by circumstances another would hardly notice.

To give a simple illustration, a person motivated to operate free from constraints can fight with all the fervor, cunning, and ethics of Jack the Ripper if you close in on him. Another person relishes definition and parameters, but can go slowly berserk if placed in a situation of conflicting priorities and working with a non-managerial boss.

Similarly, an independent person motivated to tightly control those from whom he seeks a particular response gets more and more irritated at the new boss's insistence on following, in detail, company directives. On the other hand, the person motivated to follow instructions and satisfy requirements thinks the new boss is a gift from God.

If there is such a diversity of reaction to just the factors of structure and definition, you can see the enormous possibilities for differences and criticisms given the range of other factors in a motivational pattern. What is expected of each Christian depends upon where the attention is needed, how much grace has been received, and how far down the road of spiritual maturity a person has come.

Giving Us New Choices—The Steps of Renewal

To this point we have seen that being a Christian means we address our bad habits and ways of conducting our lives by cooperating with God's work of bringing us out of our self-centered compulsions into the freedom of being who He intends us to be. His desire is that we live in full measure the heritage of being made in His image, which means that we, like Him, must be free.

Since we tend to define freedom mostly as an opportunity to do what we want to do, when we want to do it, for our good alone, God needs to replace our small liberties with His full-orbed freedom. Remember the Scripture: ''So if the Son makes you free, you will be free indeed'' (John 8:36 RSV). In this verse we get a sense of contrast between what the expert in freedom knows to be reality and our poor substitutes. The fact that we do pursue substitutes suggests that we have a capacity for genuine freedom. But to attain it, our substitutes have to go. They must be stripped away.

The stripping away process is part of sanctification, and it centers on the area of our strengths, not so much where we are weak. It is where we are gifted that God must seriously address our self-centeredness. Our gifts can be applied to fulfill the will of God in our lives, or they can be misapplied to get our own way. Our prison cells can have the same names on them as do our gifts, but once our motivational gifts have been identified, we have a means to discern when we are in prison and when we are free. This discernment is necessary because Satan can easily fool us. He deceives Christians into "doing their own thing" and glorifying self without being aware of what is actually happening.

All Christians know that "doing your own thing" is deadly, but usually associate it with hedonism. They do not see Satan operating in the area of gifts. There he tempts Christians to take on spiritual tasks or ministries that are not natural to them ("Yes, I'll be glad to teach Sunday school") and has them believing that because the goal is spiritual, God can overlook the presumption. God will not violate who He made you to be by calling you to take on a ministry or other spiritual work not in harmony with His purpose in creating you. Christ works incarnationally in your body, mind, and spirit to enable you to act out increasingly the person God created you to be. Attempting to pursue some other calling violates His creative goal for you.

That in no way means that God will *never* place us in situations where we must operate in ways inconsistent with our gifts. (Somebody has to wash the dishes and clean up after the pot luck if the people who are really good at it are not around.) Practical experience denies that. It is just that we should never expect such to be the norm. In addition, there are times when actual denial of our gifts is in God's plan, as we can see when we consider the basic steps involved in our being made a new creation in Christ.

Step one—accept God's will for you

The first step in the renewal process corresponds with the first step in the sequence of events in the passion of Jesus. When we envision Jesus in the Garden of Gethsemane, we see a man who had to face horrible events in His life, events that were part of God's plan for His life. We can be sure He hoped for another scenario, because He said, "If it be possible, let this cup pass from me" (Matt. 26:39 KJV). Sweat and blood demonstrated the intensity of the request. But Jesus went through the agony of acceptance to conclude in the same verse, "Nevertheless, not as I will, but as thou wilt." Acceptance made the monumental difference in His life, and acceptance opens the way to a difference in ours.

If we are to follow Christ, we, like Him, must yield to the place allotted to us in creation. We must give up any complaint about our lot and substitute in its place an acceptance of the Father's will. You might look at another person's gift and assume you would be happier if you had it. The reality is that such considerations are absurd. To be you is to have the gifts you have. You cannot be anyone other than who you are, and you cannot have what you are not given. "For everyone has his own proper burden to bear" (Gal. 6:5 NEB).

You may not be as beautiful or handsome or intelligent or talented as you feel you ought to be. You may be haunted by fantasies of what you wish you were and anguished over what you are not. Not only could you not be consulted about the time, place, and conditions of your birth and upbringing, but once you were brought into being, you also discovered that your potential was flawed by sin you did not initially ask for, and all your hopes were endangered by the risks of haphazard existence.

That is all true. Yet, knowing that God was not caught by surprise by man's Fall, we must conclude that we can trust whatever He is doing, not only for the world, but also for ourselves. Our energies need to be focused on God's game plan, not frittered away on wishful thinking or complaining about that which has no possibility of changing.

You can trust that eventually everything shoddy and insufficient, evil or ugly, will be dealt with. Redemption is God's aim. When we enter into God's salvation, we are brought into harmony with God's intentions, so shoddiness and insufficiency in us are to be transformed, not only at the end of the story, but beginning now.

But we need to participate with God's way. In spite of how it looks, though present circumstances may not be the way we want them, we will be satisfied by the ending of the story. We must keep that in mind as we view our immediate lives as well as our destiny. We should not argue about the motivational abilities we have discovered any more than we should argue with Him about our height or the color of our hair. "Will the pot contend with the potter, or the earthenware with the hand that shapes it? Will the clay ask the potter what he is making? or his handiwork say to him, 'You have no skill?'" (Isa. 45:9 NEB).

Considering what the eternal promises are—that we will be joint heirs with Christ, that we will put on immortality, that we will be given ecstatic experiences, that we will see God—the most minimal role we could be given in life is still a gift so astounding that we had better be grateful. Be grateful regardless of who we are. We have, at least, the incomprehensible gift, a foothold that will surely have enormous consequences.

Step two—act out who you are
Having discovered the inevitable blessing of being itself, enter into it by being, as much as possible, who and what you are. There is obviously an unfathomable mystery about how and why we are born into the process of time and the peculiarity of all the good and bad that adds up to us. There is no possibility of understanding that mystery. We ought only to respond with an unconditional acceptance of who we are and who God is.

Can the pot speak to the potter and say, "Why did you make me like this?"? Surely the potter can do what he likes with the clay. Is he not free to make out of the same lump two vessels, one to be treasured, the other for common use? (Rom. 9:20, 21 NEB).

If you have a gift that places you in front of people, do not attempt to cloister yourself and think you please God. Take your rightful place. If you have a gift to make money, do not pray that God remove it (He would have to remove you), but find a way that you can make money to give to those in need. If you have a large gift and you are a treasure in the church, do not count yourself more worthy—or if your gift is common, less worthy.

If others recognize you as a treasure, do not play games with praise, but be thankful. If you have an unrecognized gift and you conduct yourself in an unassuming way, do not allow covetousness for attention to poison the beauty God is forming in you.

Season your days and ways with prayers of yieldedness, and be who God created you to be. There is no other way you can be fulfilled. Yield to His will and become what He intends rather than what you or others desire. In the strength of the Holy Spirit, live out the Gethsemane words of Jesus.

Step three—take up your cross daily

"I am crucified with Christ: nevertheless I live; yet not I, but Christ liveth in me" (Gal. 2:20 KJV). This is one of the famous verses of the Bible, but it is at the same time a very peculiar Scripture, especially if we look at it from the logical point of view.

It states that   I am dead.
                  I am alive.
                  It is me.
                  It is not me; it is Christ—all these at the same
                  time.

It is, of course, a paradox.

The Christian enters into this paradoxical relationship with the Lord and is able to claim that when he is dead to the compulsive exercise of his gifts, God is using them. When that is our actual experience, others discover a special loveliness in our work and walk with the Lord. But again, it is only possible if our gifts are "crucified," that is, when we are willing to die to using our gifts how and when and where *we* want.

A path to Christian maturity resides in this truth. No matter how great or small the gifts, *all* gifts must be crucified. They all come from God and must all be given back to Him unconditionally. "He who finds his life will lose it, and he who loses his life for my sake will find it" (Matt. 10:39 RSV).

There are many unhappy, spiritually schizophrenic Christians who apparently gave themselves to the Lord, but their gifts and motivations did not follow. They say they desire to please

God, yet their abilities are self-centered, unyielded, and essentially unfruitful. The problem is even more painful when those gifts are large. Others see and are amazed at abilities so blatantly aimed at enlarging self, all in the pretense of serving God.

This principle not only applies to the gifts you are able to use, but also has application when circumstances prevent their exercise. There are times when our desires must be set aside for the greater fulfillment that comes when we are asked to take up our cross.

We experience crucifixion and the effective death to self when we are willing to relinquish our motivation and accept the circumstances or role, or lack of role, God chooses to give us for His sake or for the sake of another. Burning with the answer and not saying it, carrying a spear when you clearly are best for the lead, following directions you know are inefficient, giving your careful attention to someone who crosses your motivational desires—all are examples of being crucified with Christ, if, of course, you yield yourself up to Him to do what is right to Him.

That is how you take up your cross, but you do so aware of the command to follow: "If any man would come after me, let him deny himself and take up his cross and follow me" (Matt. 16:24 RSV). For Jesus Christ is moving from crucifixion and death into resurrection. In spite of the nails and the blood and the tortured, twisted body; in spite of the agony; in spite of what it looks like; there is *no* possibility of ultimate failure in God. Jesus Christ did not stay dead, nor do we. God's warning is clear and severe:

The fire will test the worth of each man's work. If a man's building stands, he will be rewarded; if it burns, he will have to bear the loss; and yet he will escape with his life, as one might from a fire (1 Cor. 3:13–15 NEB).

When that fire (God's presence) tests your work, it will be consumed—if it is ultimately yours. If it is ultimately God's (you gave it away!), it will last.

The world and the church are burdened with a parade of Christians exercising gifts having no wounds, knowing no death, bearing no scars, acting independently, as if they did not belong to a crucified Lord and did not have to walk the Via Dolorosa with Him.

When churches are preoccupied with show business, with imitating the world, with prima donnas, with names and numbers, with fame, and with crowds and recognition, they demonstrate their failure to understand that Jesus must be the attraction. He said, "If I be lifted up . . . [I] will draw all men unto me" (John 12:32 KJV). God's means of attraction is a bloody one, and any man who would honor God must share in that death; and any work that he does, any motivation he has, any accomplishment he produces, must share the same. Leave your gift on the altar and do not take it back until He gives it back.

Remember again that Scripture teaches that whatsoever you do, do it heartily as unto the Lord and not unto men (see Col. 3:23). Whatsoever—work or play, cleaning, washing, eating, living, digging, building, talking, teaching, directing, walking, driving, learning—do all of it as unto the Lord, but a crucified Lord. All of it must be crucified, for there will be no resurrection, no life, no meaning to it all without the cross.

Step four–live in the truth of resurrection

The process of sanctification is not complete in crucifixion, however. For, of course, the gospel is good news and is more extensive and far more positive than just that. The Christian story is one of life. Moreover (to use Jesus' words), it is about abundant life. And it comes to us through the resurrection of Jesus.

Because we know as Christians that this world can never really be home to us, there is a justified pessimism about the way the world goes. Yet that should not blunt our joy in the truth of the gospel that says the end of the story will be delightfully satisfying. We are to draw on that hope and involve ourselves in demonstrating in our work and witness that we are products of resurrection power. Though the exercise of our gifts and abilities takes place in the midst of a world that avidly pursues death, do not assume that the exercise is futile. We must believe that God intends to use our gifts in ways that will actually have eternal consequences for us as well as for others. What is given life by the Spirit of God lasts. That is possible for us because we are new creatures in Christ. "You must be made new in mind and spirit, and put on the new nature of God's creating" (Eph. 4:23, 24 NEB).

The question to be asked here is whether this putting on of the new man means a change in an individual's motivational pattern. Is not that part of having a new nature in Christ?

Our evidence demonstrates that motivational patterns do not change when a person becomes a Christian. The ingredients seen prior to conversion are seen after conversion. This is disturbing to people who expect it to be otherwise, but perhaps we will better understand our position in Christ if we see that God's intention for us is not *replacement* of who we are, but *redemption* of who we are. God's creation of us, including our basic motivational pattern, is not bad. What happened to us through the Fall and our subsequent evil choices is so bad that there was nothing we could do to correct it.

Redemption means bringing us back to that which God originally intended, but because of the bounty of His nature, He goes beyond mere restoration to Eden. Once lower than the angels, we are made joint heirs with Jesus Christ. Conversion has us rejoicing in the fact that we are enabled to become who we *originally* were made to be, rather than becoming someone entirely different. The renewal takes place when we are resurrected in conversion; and sanctification causes a radical change, not in the gift we have, but in its purpose and use.

Before Christ, we are motivated to excel, prevail, build visible things, overcome impossible obstacles, gain honors, pioneer new territory, have an impact on others, and so on. And the purpose, frankly, was that we might be, like God, worshiped, exalted, praised, and honored. All natural motivations lead to man's competing with God. That is our fallen nature.

After we have believed in Jesus Christ as our Lord and submitted to sanctification, we enter a process that, if allowed to continue, will gradually bring about a transformation of our motivation. Instead of exercising our motivated abilities in order to be the object of worship by others, we come into a condition of heart wherein we exercise it to please and serve the Lord. God is the welcome audience.

Step five–abide in Christ
     Over the years, the process of renewal requires that we continue to abide in Christ.

Abide in me, and I in you. As the branch cannot bear fruit of itself, except it abide in the vine; no more can ye, except ye abide in me. I am the vine, ye are the branches: He that abideth in me, and I in him, the same bringeth forth much fruit: for without me ye can do nothing (John 15:4, 5 KJV).

Therefore, since Jesus was delivered to you as Christ and Lord, live your lives in union with him. Be rooted in him; be built in him; be consolidated in the faith you were taught; let your hearts overflow with thankfulness (Col. 2:6, 7 NEB).

     When you credit God with your gifts and motivations, the new dimensions brought into your life involve the work of your hands. The daily job is where you and Christ can abide in one another. It is not just a Sunday morning matter. There is no other more spiritual life and situation where the Lord would prefer to direct His attention.
     Assuming you are in the job or role making use of His gifts, where you are is where you can especially sense He is. That is precisely where you are to work out your salvation with fear and trembling, while God is working in you, inspiring both your will and your deeds for His own chosen purpose. "For it is God which worketh in you both to will and to do of his good pleasure" (Phil. 2:13 KJV).
     What does one do to abide in Christ? Consider everything you think, taste, see, feel, hear, and do as falling within God's concern. Develop a sensitivity to the voice of God in your thoughts and to the hand of God engineering your cir-cumstances. Seek an obedient heart so that you will be quick to yield into God's hand a situation that has gotten out of control;

to act when you are responsible for deciding, even in the face of doubt and questions; to release resentment you felt when you were criticized; to be quiet in the presence of a competitor's superior wisdom; to seek His strength when the seventh day is required. Be quick to ask for help rather than bluff your way through, to seek understanding rather than react in conventional ways.

Give thanks, praise, and adoration to the One who adorns your life when judging conflicting claims, and who yesterday moved you to tears with an act so loving, so hidden in the tiny folds of your life, that no one but He could have known.

Recognize that abiding in Christ has its literal side, too. The church is the Body of Christ, and to be joined to it is essential if you expect to flourish as a Christian. Since God did not give each of us all the gifts, He made us dependent upon one another. We need each other's gifts, and we need a body of believers with leaders who are gifted to orchestrate a balanced exercise of all the gifts so *all* will flourish.

In Summary

The process of sanctification we have described (certainly a partial treatment) is enough to assist the newcomer and remind the experienced. The biblical instructions for walking in the Spirit and not in the flesh (yieldedness, taking up your cross daily, living in the resurrection life of Jesus) are basic to the process of renewal that results in the new man or new woman being formed.

But through it all, down the years of walking with the Lord, the ingredients and thrust of your design, your motivational pattern, your direction remain the same. However, as you grow up from being a babe in Christ to where your heart is broken and made soft, your thoughts are more and more resident in the beauty and grace of God. You will find you are less compulsive about how and when you make the moves we call your motivational pattern. You will experience, in place of the goading taste of desire to satisfy your motivational pattern, patience with people and circumstances that require attention, peace in the face of apparent defeat, long-suffering when blocked by frustration, a sense of joy over benefits received by others, and a surge of love for someone who cannot possibly do anything for you.

10

Ordering Your Life According to Your Gift

BEING IN A JOB OR ROLE SUITABLE FOR OUR gifts is essential in fulfilling God's will. Until the Christian is doing what he should be doing, maturation is hampered. Being in a place accommodating God's design is critical.

For most people, however, it is difficult to admit that the decisions that put them in their current jobs were not very wise and they need to make new and much better decisions to find more suitable positions. Somewhere between 50 and 80 percent of working Americans occupy jobs wrong for them, according to published surveys.

Job Misfit Is Normal?

In the teaching profession, we have found that at least two-thirds are not motivated to teach, and we have been criticized for being conservative in our estimates. Examining managers and executives, we have found that only one out of three appears well-matched to his job. Many clergy are not gifted at central requirements like preaching, teaching, and evangelism. One wonders how bad it is with waitresses, doctors, bankers, electricians, and assembly workers.

The numbers defy belief, much less precise measurement. Surely people living out years of joyless work are aware of their unhappiness. Surely they know, or at least once knew, that life must be more than a daily grind. There are those who had or who now have no other practical alternatives. That is a price millions have paid because sin still rules the hearts of those leaders who could make a difference. We see this as tragedy, to be dealt with by Christians as they would handle other losses and occasions where suffering is involved.

Being deprived of fulfillment because of family difficulties, cultural limitations, lack of education, social or political restriction, or economic hard times is a tragedy of misused human resources. It is tragic for the societies that bring them about and for each misused individual involved. But to be numbered among the unfulfilled workers when it is not necessary is sadder yet. The former may receive the rewards of martyrs, having their years of strength so misused. The latter may contemplate serious judgment for squandering their talents.

It is our purpose here to call attention to the matter of Christians faced with the possibility that they are not pursuing the vocation to which they have been called. We trust the need for finding and obeying that calling has been established in the earlier chapters, so that we can assume here that the Christian will want to and, in fact, "must order his life according to the gift the Lord has granted him" (1 Cor. 7:17 NEB).

Many, however, fail to step into the vocation to which they have been called for reasons they do not understand. They know they should be about the work of their hands but they are not, and in response to questions, they come up with excuses that, repeated often enough, nobody (including themselves) believes are true. As a result, so many lives seeking sincerely to be dedicated to the Lord fail to get off the ground vocationally, in spite of so much promise.

The "Suffering" of Artists

Inaction is frequently due to ignorance of those factors in one's motivational pattern that must be present for motivated behavior to take place. Especially does this seem true of artists, poets, and writers whose work assumes an ability to create. For many, their creative life consists of bursts of "creativity" followed by long periods of dryness, with little explanation for their production or lack of it. Failure to understand what is necessary to trigger "creativity" is cause for much anguish and frustration. Once having given birth to a work of art, doubt often remains about how "creative" it actually was.

We have worked with artists whose careers were, or had been, seriously stalled because they did not understand how their motivational patterns affected their artistic expression. Stuart, for example, was a painter who had been considered very promising by his teachers in college and graduate school. He was very productive in school, having almost always completed assignments in advance of when they were due. He was eager to establish his own studio and hoped to translate the interest his teachers had in his work into some healthy sales.

Once established in his studio, however, Stuart found himself unable to create works of art beyond imitation of what he had done in the past. He was frightened by the idea that his creative spring had dried up. So when we helped him discover his motivational pattern, we knew we were dealing with someone who had more than a casual interest in the results.

We discovered that Stuart's motivational thrust was to fulfill requirements. When taught a particular technique, he loved to fulfill its demands. When he was a given a specific assignment, he was pleased to satisfy every requirement. Had he been taught by instructors who gave open-ended assignments or who posed problems requiring creative solutions, Stuart would not have been encouraged. As it was, he had attended a school dominated by a faculty skilled in techniques and methods. Students who could reproduce those received high grades.

Obviously, a career redirection was in order. We recommended art restoration to Stuart. His high level of skill in reproducing techniques stood him well in such a field. He had first of all, however, to give up the idea of his being creative, a very difficult task in view of his fame in school. But recalling his fearful studio period forced him to be realistic about himself, and he was soon headed in the right direction.

Stuart's situation in art is similar to that of a musician we know who had suffered from many attempts to "create" new music within the musically isolated environment of a Christian fellowship. Her motivational pattern clearly revealed a central thrust to replicate established musical ideas and techniques, so a more fertile musical environment and well-equipped facilities were crucial to the pursuit of the vocation to which she had been called.

A jazz musician possessing an exciting talent had foundered in her career because she needs to work her musical ideas off those of other highly talented musicians (not available in her area), whose playing is a necessary springboard for her "creative" and fulfilling expression.

None of these artists were aware of those specific elements of their motivational pattern that had to be engaged before they could find their right place.

Most Teachers Aren't Motivated to Teach

Outside the world of the artist, there are thousands of Christians in vocations not faithful to their design simply because they are ignorant of certain critical elements of their motivational patterns. The educational world is full of such misfortunes. Consider this Christian teacher.

Barbara had seven years of experience teaching in a private secondary school for gifted students. The school was well-equipped, and the student-teacher ratio was ideal. Yet she felt that while everyone else on the faculty seemed to be pleased with having an ideal teaching situation, she was peculiarly unfulfilled. And at the end of her seventh year, Barbara was notified by her headmaster that she was being let go.

The initial shock prevented Barbara from being able to counter immediately the headmaster's reasons for the dismissal, but subsequently her defensiveness caused her to make critical statements about the lack of student response in that school. Her conclusion was that she would never teach again.

Examination of her motivational pattern revealed that she was motivated to work with people who had needs she could satisfy. All of Barbara's teaching experience, however, was with students who were remarkably free of needs, highly successful academically, and at an age where learning how to be independent is the preface to adulthood. The rare occasions when a student did come to her with a problem were especially satisfying, but such opportunities confused her understanding of job-fit.

While many of Barbara's motivated abilities could be satisfied in teaching, it was necessary that they be directed toward students who had genuine needs. Moving toward a learning disabilities specialization salvaged her credentials and her employment experience, and also revived her joy in teaching.

Often a teacher is in the wrong level or subject and does not understand what is wrong or what would be right until the motivational pattern reveals the answers to both questions. Consider these mismatches of teacher and position:

- a high school math teacher motivated to teach, but only by demonstration
- a college teacher of American history motivated to work with what is new and different
- a high school English teacher not motivated to teach but motivated to advocate
- teachers not motivated to teach but to act, to counsel, to control, or to solve problems

Pursuing Other Gods

What is true of people misplaced in the educational world has its counterpart in the world of business and industry, where ignorance of one's design guarantees a darkness of the soul.

Salespeople motivated to persuasively explain a product or concept but who are not motivated to confront or close a sale are classic examples of job misfit. "No wonder I was so miserable in selling! I never understood why until now," we have heard many say.

Of a similarly classical nature are the cases of people motivated to meet needs and fulfill requirements of others, and who rise to the top of their function or even the entire organization. At that point, the person finds he is in the wrong job, becomes increasingly uneasy, but does not understand what went wrong and why. Now he has to perform that responsibility and cannot, simply cannot.

Numerous examples emerge out of a failure to understand the absence or presence of particular subject matter in the motivational pattern. Thus we have personnel representatives not motivated to work with people, professional engineers not motivated to work with concepts, a business manager not motivated to work with numbers, or a product planner unaware that he is not motivated to work with strategies and tactics.

In a similar vein, ignorance about the motivating circumstances of the pattern can entrap an individual: the researcher who needs instructions to follow; the secretary motivated to work in an unstructured, fluid situation working for the closely supervising boss; the unhappy cost accountant not aware of the desire for visibility and notoriety in his pattern; the staff member always causing near disasters because she is unaware that risks and hazards are a circumstance of motivating value to her.

Ignorance of the motivational pattern and its constituent elements is the root cause of a large share of the tragedy among Christians who fail to claim their share of Christ's bounty.

Bending Your Neck Is Not Just an Idea

A surprisingly large number of Christians we have encountered have failed to locate and enter the vocation to which they have been called because they have been unwilling to submit themselves and their gifts to the discipline of an apprenticeship or the formal education necessary for their full expression and employment. Useful service to mankind is thereby aborted, and the gifts can only be a shadow of what might have been.

The phrase "half-baked" is apt in describing many artists, poets, musicians, entrepreneurs, preachers, counselors, and singers who seek a quick road to being equipped to perform the work of their ministry. Unfortunately, the quality of their work signals their failure to bend their necks to those tutors and governors God had appointed to bring them into maturity.

In such cases, bullet-biting means a decision to go back and build the foundation of understanding that should have been built years ago when a decision was made to skip those preliminaries. Without such a foundation, the resulting scholarship, music, literature, painting, therapy, or business ventures may get some support, but rarely is God glorified by the second-rate results.

We are not talking about form or necessarily about having or not having a college degree. We are talking about really knowing your subject if you are working with it; about carefully studying new developments critical to your field of work; about understanding the tools, techniques, and vocabulary others have established that are substantial and helpful to what you do today; and about having the amount and level of education necessary to be competent. Whatever is critical to your being equipped to be outstanding in the vocation to which you have been called by God, you should be about learning.

In evaluating a current situation that seemed to be so promising earlier, but that turned increasingly sour the deeper you got into it, suspect a failure to build the foundation of knowledge and skills really needed. If that is the case, consider the hard decision of doing what you should have done in the first place.

The flip side

Even more costly is the mistake of those who have been formally trained to follow a vocation for which they were not called and for which they are not motivationally equipped or gifted.

They go to college because that is the next expected step. They select a major because they have to select something. They look for and land a particular job for all sorts of reasons, most of them superficial.

What is true of going to college is also often true of junior college, trade school, secretarial school, and the family business. It may make sense, but in too many cases it does not. People can be equipped by their training or education to do that which they are not designed to do. If that turns out to be you, facing the reality that you may be in the wrong field of work and sacrificing what you have invested in it may be a small price compared to the fulfillment available to those who are using their vocational gifts in their work every day.

Your Education Should Develop Your Strengths

Evaluating how well my career matches my motivational pattern is not exclusively a mid-career problem. Students starting, finishing, or midway through the educational process that is supposed to equip them for the world of work share the dilemma. Am I studying what I should be studying? Am I being prepared for what God has in mind for me?

Be quite sober about taking stock. As a Christian, you have been given gifts that you are to invest wisely. You will be held by God to an accounting of what use you have made of those gifts. At that point in eternity, you will not be able to "pass the buck" to some career counselor or fast-talking recruiter. You are responsible for your own decisions, and once you have taken the large step of discovering your design, you have lost your last excuse. You know the number and kinds of talents the Lord has given you.

Step one of your evaluation process is to examine how you go about learning and what you are motivated to learn. You will find a congruity in those elements of your pattern. We mean that what you are motivated to learn will accommodate how you are motivated to learn.

For example, if you are motivated to learn by doing-trying out, the subject matter with which you are motivated to work could include items like physical or manual expression, dance, designs, and machinery. If you are motivated to learn by memorizing-repeating, likely subject matter could be language, music, logistics, and biology. If you are motivated to learn by studying-reading, probable subject matter should include principles or theories, ideas or concepts, science, people, and economics.

Now is the time to decide if your goals and methods of reaching them are compatible with your personal design motivations. If you find you are motivated to learn by doing and you are majoring in history, you are or will be in trouble. If you do not have people in your subject matter and you are majoring in clinical psychology; if you learn by memorizing and you are tackling an engineering curriculum; if money or numbers are not in your subject matter and you are majoring in economics—you have started on a road that will not lead where you want to go, and nearly as we can discern, God is not interested in what other people have in mind for you to become.

Apart from liberal arts or basic courses necessary to keep all students within the category of the civilized, your studies should be equipping you to perform the work for which you were designed. On the other hand, once your mentors understand your pattern (and you should make sure they do), you should be open to their advice about what courses will be helpful or even critical to pursuing the vocation that seems right for you. For example, if a certain amount of math is necessary to be an athletic trainer, a curriculum specialist, or a psychology major, discipline yourself to take it whether or not it fits your motivational pattern. As long as you are sure the long-range goal fits your gifts, you have enough reason to conquer the subject matter necessary to achieving those goals.

Can You Make Decisions?

While we are considering education, be aware of how many critical decisions need to be made while in school and how such decisions are affected by your motivational pattern.

If you are faced with a need to adjust or change courses, majors, or even schools, you may discover whether your motivational pattern enables or gets in the way of decision-making. You may be motivated to make decisions only in certain ways—for example, only after exhaustive gathering of data or when you can check each step with some authority. Perhaps you can only make good decisions when part of a group process, or you may not be motivated to make decisions where there are more than two options.

Whatever you pattern reveals you to be as a decision-maker, seek whatever help or mechanism is indicated by your pattern. We trust you will recognize (here and elsewhere) the need for prayer and seeking specific direction from the Holy Spirit to assist you out of your darkness into His light. Look for those in the Christian body whose gifts can be of help to you. (A seminar in decision-making will probably not help too much!)

Don't Just Look at the First Job

What is true of decision-making is true of planning. Many of us, probably most of us, are practically unable to plan a strategy for activity a few months in the future, much less several years. If you are such a person, seek help from someone available to you who has a motivated ability to plan. Ask him to help you look down the road and chart at least a tentative course to follow.

When you consider the vocation for which you are now preparing, look at it as it will presumably unfold, and not just where you start into it or a few years down the line. Be cautious if the direction you select will eventually require you to become something significantly different from what you are.

Playing Games with God

Knowing the motivational shape of your will is a critical insight to knowing whether you are deviously misusing the Lord to make, or avoid, a decision. Here are some quick introductions to people whom we have met in the past, people who could not separate the voice of God from the voice of their own motivational compulsions:

● An executive, mainly unsuited for his number two job in a company, who is motivated to acquire money, status, and material things, claims that he is not being led by the Lord to take the right job with a fledgling company and be part of a small team.

• Another executive, motivated to excel and well-suited for his current position, finds all sorts of reinforcement "from the Lord" to support a decision to uproot his family and move 1,500 miles to accept a new, higher-level position.

• A teacher, enjoying an excellent reputation and responsive students, motivated to overcome near-impossible obstacles, gets direction "from the Lord" in the middle of the term to accept an offer from a struggling school on the West Coast and joins them with one week's notice to her current employer.

• A young woman, motivated to wow others and very quick at grasping and embellishing basic concepts, decides the Lord wants her to quit fine arts school after two semesters and go out and get an art job.

• A thirty-six-year-old superintendent, not motivated to manage others, sees God directing him to a similar job after he was fired because he was a poor people manager.

• A forty-five-year-old secretary, motivated to meet requirements and fill needs but by finishing one task before starting another, sees the hand of God in an offer to become secretary to the needy president of a large, international missionary society whose office is constantly busy and in turmoil.

In none of the preceding examples are we presuming to know what the Lord had in mind. We are emphasizing the need for Christians to know their motivational tendencies and unmask and face those tendencies before they see the Lord's hand as facilitating or staying.

The Wife in the Home

Although many wives and mothers have decided to pursue careers outside the home, many women are still following the difficult vocation of homemaker. And the homemaker, like everyone else, should examine her suitability for the role she has undertaken. Does the subject matter in the pattern fit those

things you work with as a homemaker? Some? None? All? Do
you like to work with such things as home furnishings, food and
cooking, children, details, or money and budgets?

Depending upon the details of your situation, motivations
such as *explore, pioneer, overcome, prevail, meet the challenge, become proficient,* or *gain response* can find expression
at home. However, motivations like *advance, progress, gain
recognition or attention, excel, be the best,* or *be unique or
outstanding* would have a hard time finding satisfaction in the
role of homemaker-mother.

When you consider your operating relationship with others,
most types can be accommodated at home, sooner or later,
particularly if children come along. *Team members, managers,
coaches, directors,* and *commanders* can all find happiness in
the home, although some fit better than others. For example,
teaching a child to spell is preferable to directing a child to do
things the way mother did. In the evaluation process, you need
to face squarely who you are relationally, what is your husband's
way of relating to others, and your plan to have a child or
children. If the home is limiting your way of relating, much can
be done outside the home in the community and church to
exercise your way of operating with others. You can, for instance, direct a choir or organize and run a political campaign.

When you consider the circumstances aspect of your motivational pattern, most elements can fit the home situation. Those
elements you perhaps cannot introduce, such as *structure, instruction, standards-grades,* or *deadlines,* can be established
by your husband. The other common elements like *stress,
outdoors, need for cost control,* and *difficulty* are all found in
abundance at home. A few elements like *visibility, audiences,*
and *positions of status* will cause difficulty and may indicate the
need for an additional career, whether paid or voluntary, especially if those factors have related elements under abilities and
other parts of the pattern, as they likely will.

The parts of your pattern in conflict with homemaking need
not prevent you from becoming an acceptable homemaker and
mother, if it is understood that there will be a high degree of

self-denial while children are very young, and that you will need certain kinds of help from your husband. As children become older, time can be given to the beginnings of a career that is much more on target motivationally, and that can be fully entered into when the nest is empty.

Essentially the same range of possibilities is true of the abilities part of the motivational pattern. The home accommodates most abilities, except those oriented to the outside world such as publicizing, selling, and performing.

The husband has responsibility in these matters also. The biblical role for him is that of being the serving priest of the home. The wife and children are to be covered by the authority he has been given by God, regardless of whether he looks authoritative. The Scripture indicates that in that position, he is responsible for his wife's fulfillment. We see this not just in terms of daily bread or sexual needs. The husband is also to enable his wife to exercise her gifts as much as possible, even if it may mean some element of difficulty for him as a result. "Husbands, love your wives, as Christ also loved the church and gave himself up for it" (Eph. 5:25 NEB).

Christians should have disturbed the traditional roles for homemaker and breadwinner long before the world ever thought of it. As much as is possible, all the responsibilities of the home should be redistributed to match the respective gifts of husband and wife. Such redistribution should not disturb the role of husband as head of the house, nor should it permit the blurring of differences between the sexes that God designed and that make marriage so interesting.

If the wife has management skills the husband lacks, she should be given the opportunity, without violating the husband's position, to take on those areas in the home that require such a gift—for example, the care and feeding of the budget or investment of savings, or planning an extended vacation. If the wife has elements in her pattern that lend themselves to positions of authority, she should discover opportunities to use them outside the home—for example, running the church school program or a daycare facility. The authority of the husband should not be a matter of him striving against his wife in order to maintain it. It is a matter so critical to the well-being of the family and the self-identity of the children that both man and wife should be zealous in support of his authority.

"Wives, be subject to your husbands, as to the Lord. For the husband is the head of the wife as Christ is the head of the church" (Eph. 5:22, 23 RSV).

Submission of the wife to the husband is not based on whether she is more or less intelligent or more or less gifted than the husband. It is based on the fact that we all need to submit in order to have spiritual health. God is not asking the wife to do any more than He is asking of the husband. In fact, the husband is required to know more of submission than does the wife. He is to submit to Christ's standard of being a husband, loving his wife "as Christ loved the church and gave himself up for her" (i.e., *died* for it; Eph. 5:25 RSV).

Prickliness about the word *submission* can be removed by placing it in the context of love. After all, in both cases, we are not being asked to submit to a military commander but to the One who loves us.

Parable of the Talents—What Is Your Excuse?

Most Christians need to be pushed or nudged by God through engineered, confronting circumstance, or otherwise enticed, from darkness into the light of what He has in store for us. In reaction, many look to discover their own excuses for ignoring God's will to add to all those supplied by the world.

You may recall in the parable of the talents (Matt. 24:14–30) how the one-talent servant came up with excuses when confronted by his lord for an accounting. Here are some of the modern-day equivalents given to justify a failure to make a career move that would fully utilize one's talents: "But the kids love their school." "Blanche worries about losing all those benefits." "We go to such a fine church." "I love the seasons so." "Harriet's parents live nearby." "We have such nice neighbors." "It would be tough to begin lower down the ladder." "But I've got tenure." "I've gotten many compliments on my teaching." "Perhaps when I retire." "Perhaps if I were younger." "I've been an elder so long." "I don't know anything about the area." "We would need two cars." "I'd have to make up for a lot of lost time." "I'm sure I would take a real cut in pay." "How could we do it?" "What would people think?" "Our roots are here." "It would be such a risk."

There are times to take the leap of faith from the known to the unsure and the new. For some of us, because of what we have salted away in our treasure, that step is like jumping off one of the World Trade Center towers.

Psychological Excuses: It Was Mother's Fault

A surprising number of Christians fail to make basic career decisions because they spend years dealing with what they have been told are psychological problems they must learn to overcome. As a result, they fail to evaluate the rightness of their current jobs in terms of who they are and what they want to accomplish. They see themselves as handicapped by a psychological net that, once thoroughly explored, will permit assessment and perhaps change.

Examples of such "problems" we have unearthed in our Christian clients include these common ones:

• *Problem:* I get all tense and upset when I'm in a new group. I hardly know what to say and cannot relate to them and what they are doing.

Analysis: Face the fact that your design has you exerting influence one on one by conversationally opening up another person to your thoughts and involvement with you. The group situation rarely allows you to begin to move that way because of the numbers of people, the difficulty of controlling the flow of conversation, and the relative superficiality of the conversation. No wonder you get tense.

• *Problem:* My father was always afraid to let us kids do anything risky or even new. As a result, I developed an inferiority complex and am hesitant about entering into new ventures or relationships.

Analysis: Your achievement experiences reveal a motivation to prevail over others or be better than they are. You have entered into a considerable variety of new ventures and relationships where you were outstanding or dominant. Your unwillingness to move is a selective matter. You only venture forth with a person with whom, or under circumstances in which, you perceive you will prevail or excel.

• *Problem:* I have almost a fetish about making and saving money. The reason for my compulsion is that we were very poor and I was brought up in the Depression years. That is why I will not take the risk of looking for a new job.

Analysis: You were making and saving money before you knew how to talk. No one in the family asked you to. You have a spendthrift brother and sister whose motivational patterns reflect no interest in money—making it, saving it, or spending it.

• *Problem:* My parents never encouraged me in my efforts or told me how much they loved me. As a result, I am insecure and require a lot of attention and stroking. That is why I keep changing jobs.

Analysis: You were entertaining company when you were three years old; you were on the radio when you were six; you won a popularity contest when you were nine; you had the lead in every school play throughout your high school and college years. None of your three brothers or sisters reports your problem. You just love and are at home in the limelight.

• *Problem:* My father left my mother when I was ten years old, and I had to help my mother take care of the house and help raise my brothers and sisters. As a result, I feel deprived of my childhood and particularly bitter about my father. It has ingrained in me a proclivity to serve others despite my feelings.

Analysis: If you will examine your achievement experiences, you will note you were serving others (and nurturing your dog, your paper route, and a small flock of chickens) before you were ten years old. You serve others because you are motivated to serve others. Didn't you even wonder why your brothers and sisters didn't do much serving? After all, you were only next to the oldest.

• *Problem:* My mother and father were always very protective of my brothers and me. We were never allowed to do things on our own. Because of this, I was unable to express myself in as free and creative a way as I believe I am capable of. As a result, I feel I am psychologically handicapped.

Analysis: The freedom and nature of your creativity is expressed from age four in essentially the same way, under the same conditions and mechanisms, and with the same kind of creativity at one time as at another—before you were aware of parental protectiveness, during, and afterward.

• *Problem:* My brother was much better at sports than I was and got all the attention and most of the glory. As a result, I became highly individualistic, and I dislike being with a group of people engaged in some common effort.

Analysis: Since you are the oldest child, you need to look at the fact that you were functioning as an individualist in your achievements long before your brother achieved notoriety in sports. In addition, notice that you have always preferred individual sports like tennis and skiing, and he prospered in team sports like football and basketball. Groups don't do anything for you except smother your individual effort.

• *Problem:* My sister was prettier than I was. As a result, I was very jealous of her and competed with her every chance I could get. It left me with a feeling of inferiority and always trying to prove myself.

Analysis: Your motivation is to prevail over opposition. If you will review your achievements, you will see that you competed and sought to prevail against every person and force who threatened to stand in your way. Your sister was only one example in a long line of examples.

As we mentioned earlier, when we have psychological problems, we should swiftly address the matter and get help. But we should not assume a neurosis where none exists. There are enough genuine psychological problems to be dealt with in life without adding to them unnecessarily. Living in a psychologically sensitive culture, we as Christians need to be careful about exploiting our environment to excuse our failure to move in faith. We either trust that God will take care of us, or we don't. Remembering that He clothes the lilies and feeds the sparrows will help us move out of the false security of man's systems and into the security of God.

A failure to trust God is a serious matter that should be attended to immediately. Otherwise, all you will bring into eternity is a shrunken soul barely grasping life, much less bearing loads of fruit.

Spiritualizing Our Patterns

Necessary career moves can also be avoided by the self-deceptive practice of fabricating a spiritual principle that says you can't do what you don't want to do. This self-deception can be especially difficult to recognize because it stems from one's motivational pattern.

Let us illustrate what we mean here with an example. A change that would involve investing money could be resisted by the person motivated to acquire money as risky and a violation of the Lord's admonitions to be prudent stewards of the resources given to us. His reasoning that way may be false spiritualizing, because the Lord specifically alerts us in the parable of the talents to the desirability of taking investment risks with the talents given to us (Matt. 25:14–30).

We need to be spiritually discerning and familiar with the voice of the Holy Spirit so that we can perceive the presence of theological camouflage, as in the preceding example. For the same reason, we need to invite the intervention of others in the Body of Christ to keep us on the right path. Mature brothers and sisters in Christ can provide a balanced approach in making decisions, especially those which, because of our motivational pattern, seem to us to be radical decisions. The ministry of the church in this way is a critical matter.

Edith is a mother of four grown children and a good example

of spiritualizing one's pattern. She was clearly successful as a mother, because she had weathered all the storms of such a role with the realization that her son and daughters had all been well-established in their own marriages and careers, as well as in their spiritual growth. She looked forward to extending her success into the role of a grandmother. But she was deeply troubled by her husband, Frank, a civil engineer who was seriously considering and praying about a job offer in South America. Near to retirement, he thought that his remaining work years could be a bridge to volunteer missionary work suitable to his abilities. Edith's and Frank's long and happy marriage was being disturbed by arguments, but arguments skillfully couched on both sides in "spiritual principles."

Frank took a formidable position in his feeling that the Lord was calling him to eventual "full-time service." Edith made an eloquent case for staying where they were for the cause of love, service, family, and motherhood. She pointed out that they both had, over the years, been a good teaching team in the church's marriage and family classes. Their personal experience was a rich resource for those in need of such training, and as Edith expressed it, Frank had to concur. It was no small ministry.

We suggested that Edith's intention to maintain the status quo rested primarily on the satisfaction of her motivational pattern to meet needs. The passion of her position depended on her insistence to exercise her gifts on her terms. Couldn't she do what she was gifted at doing in South America? Surely her gifts were not to be restricted to her own family? Were her priorities scriptural?

Facing the Tough Questions

Once the camouflage is peeled away, the tough questions become clear and can be dealt with. Edith wanted to stay at home. There are victims of their own patterns who want to do the reverse: overcomers from Hoboken who receive beckonings to lay the pipeline in Alaska in mid-winter; excellers who will move anywhere at any time if it is for a chance to get ahead one or, preferably, two more rungs; fulfill-requirements people who will do anything and move anywhere the boss wants; make-the-grade sergeants who have taken sight on the officers' club located in headquarters; or the challengers who just heard the San Francisco management job is open. Lust for what feeds us can transform what is holy labor into ugly striving and lead even Christians to become driven people.

No formula is available to determine what ought to be done, but the Word, the Spirit, and the Body should be enjoined in a decision. To make a right decision requires us to identify our motivational pattern and face squarely our propensity to turn away from a coming change, or to devour it and look for more.

Making decisions in such awareness helps prevent the enemy from confusing us. If the decision is one that means the denial of our motivated gifts, we can trust that God will exploit that sacrifice and eventually bring us to where we can do what He has created us to do. If the decision is one that directly opens opportunities for our gifts, we can participate without guilt. Either way, facing the knowledge of how we are motivated and praying and opening ourselves to the ministry of others is a balanced approach for finding God's will.

11

A Charge to Keep— Don't Sell or Trade It

CROSSROADS CONFRONT US THROUGHOUT OUR journey. Daily we make decisions to live or not to live in harmony with God and enjoy His provisions. While still in our youth, we are expected to make critical educational decisions. When we come of age, we decide on careers and frequently embark on climbing up some ladder of success, every rung of which requires a decision.

At each crossroad, the Christian can choose life and its resplendent joy; or he can choose to conform to the patterns of this present world and look out for "number one." In this chapter, we will examine how being of the world literally steals the joy of the Lord from the Christian. "Adapt yourselves no longer to the pattern of this present world, but let your minds be remade and your whole nature thus transformed" (Rom. 12:2 NEB).

Worldly Traps

A sampling of "the pattern of the present world" reveals a series of traps that have succeeded in snaring all but spiritually wary and mature saints.

Becoming somebody

Twisted in its perversity and cancerous in its pervasiveness is the worldly doctrine that people can be made into what the world wants. And in every field of human endeavor, there are idealistic models of behavior on which to focus our efforts.

Whether it is the model of a mom for all seasons; a clear-thinking, decision-making, compassionate executive; a dad for all seasons; a sexy, selfless, interesting wife; scientists who are good businessmen; businessmen who are creative; or a minister for all situations—we are surrounded by magazines, books, and people who insist we can develop into their models.

From grade school through high school and college and on into our careers, we strive to become somebody, some ideal. Inevitably that somebody is different from who we are already. Usually, we aim at becoming something without ever taking the time to find out who we are already. This philosophy of life is found in education, for example, where most teachers are not motivated to teach. It is also found in restaurants, in government, in the arts. Yes, it is found in the church.

Trying to become an image is wrong, whether that image is secular or spiritual. Jesus Christ has freed us from conforming to any model. We are new creatures, already designed for glory, and we need to get about the business of living out the design that is at the core of our lives.

What have you been trying to become? A realistic assessment would probably show that what you might have done is one or a combination of two things. You have been swallowed up by the world and its system and values, and you spend your life trying to become someone that people will look up to. Or you have fallen victim to a false piety in which you deny God's design and purpose for your life. You say things like "I'm nothing—I have nothing —I am unable." Here you seek to find a sanctified holiness in being either as close to zero as you can sink to or, what is even more idolatrous, trying to be something you are not and expecting God to change His mind about what He wants you to be.

Being of the world is deadly. Trying to become something or somebody is exhausting. Even if you are successful, anxious toil devastates your relationship with God. It destroys your body, infects your soul. Taking seriously the idea that you can reshape yourself to meet the expectations of man is a free pass to a phony world. Blaming others in order to shake off your badness is a ploy and only delays accountability. Convincing yourself at root that you mean good for others is self-deceit.

Moving from one teaching to another while trying to find God's will for your life; alternating between a hair shirt and a bikini in your uncertainty about lifestyle; plunging into vocation or avocation without regard to your ability to produce real craft; volunteering out of guilt; looking to someone else to make your decisions; expecting God to drop a message from the sky; doing what is difficult for you in order to increase your reliance on God; withdrawing from the world God gave His most precious possession to save—these are not exactly the victorious lives Jesus Christ had in mind, at least for most of us.

Too many lead lives fractured into secular and spiritual. Hundreds of Christians in every community do not know who they are, what they are doing, or what they are supposed to be doing with their lives. Thousands of brothers and sisters in Christ bear fruit in their work lives, family lives, and church lives that is neither tasty, graceful, lovely, nor life-giving.

What is true of the individual Christian is true of the church. Too many churches are dull and irrelevant because the pastor and the board do not know who they are, how they are to organize and function, and what contribution they are supposed to be making. Too many churches are unbalanced because they are imprinted with the passion of a strong leader who neither knows how to nor is willing to look at the design parameters of his ministry, his propensity for distortion and overreaching, and the need to surround himself with balancing, complementary strengths.

The worldly idea of becoming "somebody" is to be rejected by the Christian. And the corrective is to look to Jesus as our model, but not in an attempt to duplicate His gifts or ministry. We should use Him as an example of one who entered fully into the specific role He was given by the Father. In like manner, we should endeavor to enter fully into the specific role we have been given by the Father, accepting both our gifts and our limitations and rejoicing in fulfilling the Father's will for us.

Onward and upward success philosophy

A variation on the "becoming somebody" trap is the philosophy that says success is taking the road that leads ever higher than you are now. By this theory, workers should strive to be foremen, foremen should strive to be supervisors, supervisors should strive to be plant managers, plant managers should strive to be division managers, division managers should strive to be vice presidents, and vice presidents should strive to be presidents.

Why? If you are designed to manage, fine; you will be good at it, up to a certain level of capability. But if you are not gifted at managing, what do you think will happen to your joy and your peace if you move up that road? What about ministers with small churches? Secretaries with small offices? Teachers in rural schools?

Tragically, most who venture beyond their gifts are never willing or psychologically able to find their way home again. Even when confronted by obvious failure to perform as a department head, school superintendent, or union officer and fired from their jobs, guess what kind of job they will again seek to find.

When organizations promote such a philosophy of success, they reap the reward for their blindness in scores of job-fit nightmares, people problems, and a negative impact on their profitability.

For the Christian, that philosophy is loaded with dire implications of the bankrupt stewardship of his gifts and worshiping the false gods of success. To leave a job fully engaging God's gifts in order to ascend to a position requiring what is not possessed is treacherous.

If you are unable to use God's gifts in the new position, the demands foreign to your creation build up stress and anxiety that, if continued, will ultimately tear down your physical, emotional, and mental well-being. It quickly eats away at your relationship with God and will leave you empty-handed when you are asked to account for how you have used your share of Christ's bounty.

But when we accept God's standards of success and ambition, it is a different matter. Moving in harmony with Him, we find renewed energy in hard work; we discover health in our labors and sweetness in our advances.

The Almighty Dollar

The almighty dollar is another manifestation of the patterns of this world for which we need spiritual awareness if we are to keep it in right perspective.

God's ways and wisdom are staggering when it comes to the details of life. Here He gives each of us good gifts that, if developed and disciplined properly, can yield rewards more than ample for our needs on this earth. In fact, to the extent that we pour out His gifts in our calling, we likely will be rewarded by those we serve.

Beyond a certain point, the dollar, as such, is not of motivating value to most people. Probably less than 10 percent want to make money because they are gifted at making money. Most of us see the dollar as evidence of something—our excelling, making the grade, gaining a response, improving ourselves, advancing, or as a reward for a job well done—or as the means to buy what will impress others, realize some role or image, make the team, bring something to fruition, or build a structure.

Realizing where the dollar fits into your motivational pattern should help you deal better with its acquisition and management. It is possible to bring money into a right relationship with you, your pattern, and God's expectation.

Job-hopping as a Way of Life

There are many motivational patterns over a period of time that are not readily accommodated, given the way most organizations are managed. Even large companies, government agencies, and educational complexes fail to manage consistently most of their human resources in a way satisfying to the employee as well as productive to the organization. Managers do not actively manage their human resources unless the quality of people management is directly measurable as contributing to critical, bottom-line results. Apart from that fact, a concern for the other person is not perceived as a value of high priority, except in those managers who have such a concern in their motivational pattern or in their values.

This obvious fact of life causes special problems for people with certain designs. The person motivated to cause dramatic improvements in operating results by engineering and implementing systems and controls essentially runs out of a job after he has done his thing. Unless there are similar challenges not too far down the road this individual has the choice of moving on or holing up. A similar problem awaits the builder, the overcomer, the pioneer. A very similar problem awaits the mother who has been well-suited for her role and then watches her grown children leave home.

Problems more solvable than the preceding, but formidable still, are those that await people motivated to get on top of a challenge. Once the challenge has been met, the achiever starts looking around for the next can of worms, and he frequently will find it with another organization. Another example is that of a person who seeks to become proficient and to demonstrate competence at a new skill or a new machine. Once the new task has been mastered, this achiever starts looking around, for he has a large appetite for new avenues of learning.

All those who so work their way out of a job suitable for them face difficult choices as long as they are employed by organizations that do not accommodate their design, except from time to time. Any Christian in such a position, and there are many we have worked with, needs to be especially mindful of such implications. And he should seek a position, when the opportunity comes, where he can regularly give what God has given him to give.

Our recommendation is to talk to your boss (or potential employer) about your motivational pattern and your tendency to exhaust the challenge of a job, and frankly discuss the longer term. Usually a variety of opportunities emerge over a relatively short period of time, even in smaller organizations, that can be used to make more productive use of the gifts available in employees. The key is a desire to do so by your management.

The Unpleasant Co-worker

Many individuals who undertake to evaluate their careers are going to conclude wrongly that their jobs do not match their designs, not realizing that a certain supervisor or boss is what makes life difficult, if not downright miserable. However, because our relationship with others occupies at least half the second commandment, that is, love your neighbor, we dare not bolt from a job for a relationship reason without much extra effort and prayer.

Assuming other critical requirements of a job suit you well, it is possible that the thorn of a particular person in your life is no accident, and you had best be about learning whatever the Lord seeks to teach through it. Just a few vignettes taken from the lives of several Christian clients will make the point clear.

• You like to "wing it"; but your boss is insisting on more thorough preparation, because accuracy and impression are important to her.

• You like to be told what is wanted and then to be let alone to get the job done. Your new boss insists on riding herd over every paragraph you type to make sure you are dotting every *i* and crossing every *t*.

• Your boss swears at you. Your boss is unreasonable. Your boss insists you work a lot of Saturdays. Your boss never makes himself clear and then criticizes how you do something. Your boss always takes credit for your good suggestions. Your boss has impossible standards. Your boss is always needling you. Your boss never pays any attention to you. Your boss gets too personal. Your boss never gives you a chance to grow. Your boss expects too much from you.

The relationship factor of your pattern is very important, and we do not encourage people to take jobs that present relational difficulties if it is not necessary. But as Christians, we are also aware that there is a continuing drama going on between people, with serious, eternal consequences at stake. That fact should have a sobering effect on our attitudes, especially in view of the resources we have in Christ as we contend for the possibility of additions to the Kingdom. The job is an obvious stage for evangelism, for in the camaraderie of work, we earn the right to be heard, and there is where we display the joy of doing what we are gifted by God to do.

Here is also the place for pouring oil on the water. You are familiar with the complaints: "I can't get the night shift up to quota." "I can't get the president to buy the equipment I need." "Nobody appreciates the sacrifices I make for them." "Two of my people have gone with a competitor in the last six months." "No one wants to stick their neck out." "Nobody ever comes up with any new suggestions." "I'm so sick of bickering among the staff." "I'm sure my best salesperson is after my job." "I don't get any respect." Each such complaint is a place for action or intercessory prayer on the part of the Christian.

You may have experienced personally some of the following interpersonal unpleasantries: "It is so hard to make friends in this department." "You are nobody unless you came from the Texas plant." "The engineers in the design section will never accept my work without questioning it." "Why does accounting always doubt my expense reports?" "I honestly believe the principal intentionally made our schedule difficult." "Why does the car pool always have to wait for Charlie?" "I think they are talking behind my back." "Why do they always blame me?" "They make you feel stupid." "He makes you look foolish." "My students are so rebellious."

Difficulties with people can make a job miserable, that you otherwise really enjoy. That would justify complaint. However, each case is a matter of people coming together and is ideally supposed to be an opportunity for Christ to be in the midst of them. But if the two or three are not gathered in His name, you who bear the name cannot assume you are to take the position of any complaining worldling. You should always make use of any situation for the sake of love and the Kingdom.

Look to the Lord in each case to discover how you should replace the way you want to move with the way you ought to move, even when the gathering involved is just you and your boss.

A Charge to Keep

Losing your joy to the world is an offense to God, for, like Adam, you have a calling. You are not the result of mindless circumstance or a relentless law of cause and effect. God has summoned you into being for His chosen purpose, and He has designed you to be uniquely able to fulfill that purpose and to have joy in it.

God desires for you to bear eternal fruit through your calling. We do not presume to know the exact nature of that harvest, but we do know it will be true to your gifts, and it will yield joy, peace, and righteousness. Do not let this business about calling and joy remain a theological idea, but translate it into practical experience. Scripture urges you to do so:

Having gifts that differ according to the grace given to us, let us use them (Rom. 12:6 RSV).

Only, let every one lead the life which the Lord has assigned to him, and in which God has called him (1 Cor. 7:17 RSV).

For we are his workmanship, created in Christ Jesus for good works, which God prepared beforehand, that we would walk in them (Eph. 2:10 RSV).

I therefore, a prisoner for the Lord, beg you to lead a life worthy of the calling to which you have been called (Eph. 4:1 RSV).

We cannot love God with all our heart, mind, and strength, nor can we love our fellow men, except through the gifts with which we have been endowed and the calling or deeds for which those gifts are uniquely suited.

This is not an option. It is required performance. Finding your calling is not an abstraction reserved for the more conscientious and committed seminarians. It is foundational to any life seeking to build on and abide in Jesus Christ.

And what does a person do if he is in a job that does not fit his gifts and must stay there for reasons with which everyone would agree—for example, the prolonged ill health of a spouse? Assuming that staying in such a position is not evidence of a lack of faith or courage and is a circumstantial must, as Christians we need to recognize the situation as a call to suffering. Such day by day suffering is not dramatic martyrdom. It is, nevertheless, a form of laying down one's life for another, and it has been done and is being done by thousands. Such sacrifice Jesus Christ understands by experience in that He set aside what He was gifted to do in order literally to lay down His life for all of us. As Christ experienced joy in sacrificial love, so, too, will those Christians who sacrificially remain in unfulfilling jobs for the sake of those they love. They should look for opportunities outside their jobs to apply their gifts, perhaps in the church, community, or at home, but some place where they, too, can know they are gifted by God.

When we are given a burden to bear, we ought to bear it without complaint. In fact, we should expect God to transform it as the burden of the cross was transformed for Jesus. The serious stuff of Christianity is that we each have a burden to bear, and we must not avoid it. We are not, however, to take on that which the Lord has not given. God is not pleased for us to eat stones when He has given bread, or for us to seek pain when He offers joy.

12

Spiritual Gifts and Natural Gifts

DURING OUR TRAVELS THROUGH THE UNITED
States, in giving workshops and speaking to various Christian
groups, we discover a high level of interest in spiritual gifts
expressed in the kinds of questions we are asked. The nature of
our work easily stimulates discussion about the subject.

And there should be interest in spiritual gifts, since the New
Testament church was propelled into visibility by their use. The
results of exercising such abilities demonstrated to the world
that the church was a force with which to contend. The history
of the church since then demonstrates that there is a strong
correlation between the use of spiritual gifts and church growth.
The contemporary church in South America has retaught the
church in North America that fact.

The Scriptures do not allow us to become rigid about the
matter of gifts. If everything about the subject were so clear,
there would not be such disparate totals in the number of
spiritual gifts that have been catalogued in various books about
the subject, nor would there be so much contention among
Christian teachers and preachers about their function and how
they are received.

The contention has not served the church well. We do not
criticize an attempt to arrive at some degree of orthodoxy within
a given Christian body, but we believe it to be presumptuous to
create a degree of specificity that the Bible itself avoids, or to
make an emphasis of something in teaching scriptural truths that
the Bible does not emphasize. We need to have a sense of
proportion in dealing with these matters. Doctrinal mistakes

about spiritual gifts cannot come even close to the disaster that occurs in doctrinal errors about the divinity of Christ, for example, so we should not treat both with the same degree of passion, as if the Bible did not emphasize one more than the other.

Whatever we conclude about gifts, we personally have found it most useful for our thinking to recognize and work out two main principles that create some degree of polarity if not paradox.

The paradoxical condition was at the heart of our discussion of sanctification as we attempted to resolve the matter of grace and works. It is also in the truth that in being crucified with Christ we are dead, but also living. Paradox reappears in marriage, where partners are "one flesh," and again in the Trinity, where three Persons are one Person. It is impossible to completely resolve any of these matters, for the power of their vitality issues from the paradox itself.

To examine the paradox of spiritual gifts, we are going to exploit Friedrich Nietzsche, of all people. He was a German philosopher who vainly attempted to make God in his own image. But he is useful in that borrowing from Greek mythology, he compared the Dionysian element in man with the Apollonian. The first is that of joy in action, of ecstatic emotion, inspiration, and lively adventure. The Apollonian, in contrast, was logical order, harmonious, and balanced in, character.

One could well argue for either expression as being the best as a dominant quality, for there is good in both. However, the noblest personality in ancient Greece was neither one nor the other but a union of the two. Perhaps this might be a useful approach in the understanding of spiritual gifts, so we shall consider this division and synthesis.

Logical Order in Spiritual Gifts

The Bible does not have a strong, categorical division of gifts into spiritual and natural. In fact, in some Scriptures it looks as if the writer could be considering either. We see evidence of much that logically proceeds out of the natural in man in a continuum of harmony and order from the natural to the spiritual. The base of this position is seen in the Old Testament, where the Holy Spirit moved in the lives of individuals, on unique occasions, in a way that used as a foundation the natural gifts already in evidence. Here are some examples:

• Before Solomon prayed for and received a gift of wisdom (see 1 Kings 3:9–12), he already was considered by David, his father, to have a natural gift of wisdom (see 1 Kings 2:6, 9).

• Moses had the ability and motivation to function as a ruler and judge of the Israelites, yet he did not attempt to do so before God apprehended him and anointed him to lead His people out of Egypt (Ex. 2:11–14 compared with Acts 7:22–28).

• Daniel and his three friends had the gift of wisdom, were proficient in science, and were generally knowledgeable (see Dan. 1:4) before God gave Daniel an extraordinary opportunity to exercise understanding in all "visions and dreams" (Dan. 1:17). Notice how God gave them ten times more wisdom and understanding than the magicians and astrologers (see Dan. 1:20).

• Joseph had the gift of interpreting dreams and visions as a teenager (see Gen. 37:5–11) years before the Spirit of God enabled him to interpret the Pharaoh's dream and those of his fellow inmates (see Gen. 40, 41). Joseph said, "Not I, but God, will answer for Pharaoh's welfare" (Gen. 41:16 NEB), which is a fine definition of a spiritual gift.

• God often selected those who already had the natural ability and motivation to provide particular services and gave them a supernatural abundance of the same ability. For example, "Every wise hearted man, in whose heart the LORD had put wisdom, even every one whose heart stirred him up to come unto the work to do it" (Ex. 36:2 KJV). Samson had enormous natural strength, but he was given supernatural strength (see Judg. 14:6,19; 15:14).

The same kind of evidence exists in the New Testament,

where the natural will of man is to be used along with logical practice to get the spiritual gift functioning.

But solid food is for the mature, for those who have their faculties trained by practice to distinguish good from evil (Heb. 5:14 RSV).

I now remind you to stir into flame the gift of God which is within you through the laying on of my hands (2 Tim. 1:6 NEB).

I will pray as I am inspired to pray, but I will also pray intelligently (1 Cor. 14:15 NEB).

Do not neglect the spiritual endowment [gift] you possess, which was given you, under the guidance of prophecy, through the laying on of the hands of the elders as a body (1 Tim. 4:14 NEB).

It is interesting to consider in the latter verse the need for guidance by the Holy Spirit to pray for those gifts that fit the person. All of this speaks of balance and a clear affirmation of logical order in spiritual things, in which the natural in man is affirmed and can be affirmed since it has been aligned with the purposes of God.

There are many who would be pleased if we could conclude the matter here, but the norm we use for judgment cannot be our motivation, temperament, or inclination. We must use biblical norms, and as embarrassing as it may be to many, even a cursory reading of the New Testament clearly reveals in the area of spiritual gifts that we are dealing with dynamic power.

Inspiration in Spiritual Gifts

The mark of the Spirit's activity in the church is an explosive demonstration of mighty acts (Rom. 15:18; 2 Cor. 12:12); more than that, it even involves ecstasies (2 Cor. 12:1–7).

Dramatic healings, prophecy, discernment, sacrificial love, exorcism, speaking in tongues, and judgment of such wisdom and severity that it brings about death (all of it so extraordinary that it has been called *charismata*) are the evidences of divine power that mark the church as the true people of God.

This new splendor of the Holy Spirit reflected by the church replaces the shekinah (presence of God) in the Old Covenant. It goes beyond the wonder of God's presence in the Holy of Holies of the Jewish tabernacle and, therefore, cannot be in any degree less dramatic. In fact, relating the Christian to the Jewish covenant is a recurring biblical theme. "And you, my brothers, like Isaac, are children of God's promise" (Gal. 4:28 NEB). "For the same God who said, 'Out of darkness let light shine', has caused his light to shine within us, to give the light of revelation—the revelation of the glory of God in the face of Jesus Christ" (2 Cor. 4:6 NEB).

The operation of the Holy Spirit in the New Covenant is quite a showy display and of such quality that His witness must be clear to the church and especially to the world. God is at work.

So there we are. We cannot consider spiritual gifts without seeing their connection to natural gifts. But we cannot expect the evidence of spiritual gifts in operation to look merely like the exercise of natural gifts with theological content.

Synthesis

As every man hath received the gift, even so minister the same one to another, as good stewards of the manifold grace of God. . . . let him do it as of the ability which God giveth: that God in all things may be glorified through Jesus Christ, to whom be praise and dominion for ever and ever (1 Pet. 4:10,11 KJV).

The gifts of the Spirit differ from the natural since they require the Holy Spirit to come into a situation in a unique way. The spiritual gift cannot be expressed by natural power alone but requires that content and direction come from the Holy Spirit. That is not to say that the will of the person exercising the gift is bypassed. The exercise requires the individual's participation through the use of natural abilities, but nothing is accomplished without the specific, direct involvement of the Holy Spirit.

The Holy Spirit does not violate human will in order for a gift to be exercised. The operation of a spiritual gift is in total opposition to the exercise of demonic "gifts," in which, as in occult practices and seances, the "gifted" person shelves his will in order to become a vehicle, a puppet of spirits. In the exercise of a spiritual gift, the Christian must exercise his will or nothing real will take place. The Christian's will is not exercised abstractly, nor can it be exercised in passivity. It is exercised by acting, in this case by using natural gifts to which the Holy Spirit imparts inspiration beyond that which could be attained in the natural by itself. This is, of course, a repetition of how God has acted in the past when the body of a man was inhabited by God, ending with very man and very God simultaneously. In the use of a spiritual gift, it is clear that an individual man or woman is exercising abilities he or she has. It is equally clear that God is manifestly involved.

The natural gift cannot go beyond the rational or intuitive capacity of the mind. The spiritual gift, however, allows one to transcend reason in order to grasp mystery or revelation. The exercise of a spiritual gift thus may go beyond reason without being irrational, since it may depend upon reason in order to express something of its content.

There is much health in understanding both kinds of gifts when we realize that God is the giver of both natural and supernatural gifts. We have never seen nor can we understand God's giving a supernatural gift of the Spirit that is not at least in harmony with, if not an extension of, a person's natural gifts. Why would God violate His own creation by giving a supernatural gift to someone without the natural ground for its expression? Sometimes a spiritual gift is exercised in spite of psychological problems that would otherwise inhibit, sometimes in spite of emotional difficulties or fears, but probably not in spite of who the person was to begin with.

All we have written about natural gifts being exercised independently is true about spiritual gifts. Your gifts, spiritual and natural, should function in the context of a body of Christians who know you well, for their benefit. They should confirm your gift, help in its discipline, and nurture its growth and use. Both kinds of gifts can be misused, and both need discipline. A mature body of believers can prevent us from making the mistake of either emphasizing natural ones for fear of those that are supernatural, or cloaking natural gifts in the guise of the spiritual. Timely, effective use of gifts will prevent that dreadful phenomenon—the dead church.

It is well known that the great chapter on love in the Bible (1 Cor. 13) is sandwiched between chapters on spiritual gifts. It is also common knowledge that love is both giving and receiving. You can only give out of what you have. You love others through your gift. You also love others by not exercising your gift in order to allow others to exercise theirs. Love requires that you extend or withhold according to what *ought* to happen, not according to your wants. The Christian body made up of individuals concerned about such lovely wisdom in timing becomes a body sensitive about the effectiveness and lovingness of its ministries. There is no more attractive community in existence, as its resultant growth demonstrates. Guaranteed in all of this is joy and abundant life—there is no boredom in such a body of believers.

13

You Cannot Make It Alone

Need to be part of an effectionate functioning body of Christ

OUR INTENTION HERE IS TO PRESS HOME THE wisdom and necessity for any Christian, seeking to fulfill God's calling for his life, to be part of an effectively functioning body of Christians. Not only does the New Testament clearly establish that idea, but it also establishes the central role that gifts have in the functioning of such a body.

Can't be an island

Rather, speaking the truth in love, we are to grow up in every way into Him who is the head, into Christ, from whom the whole body, joined and knit together by every joint with which it is supplied, when each part is working properly, makes bodily growth and upbuilds itself in love (Eph. 4:15, 16 RSV).

Abiding in Christ requires abiding in His earthly Body. It is practically impossible, and theologically doubtful, for the Christian to abide and grow in Christ without being an active member of a small group of believers who function in accordance with the Scripture.

We cannot alone together

The word *alone* means not only alone by yourself, but also includes being in a church in which the body is not functioning in a scriptural manner, and in which you essentially go it alone together.

There are many forms that a valuable fellowship can take. It might be the total church experience. It may be a fellowship group or groups within a larger church body. It could emerge from a parish or a meeting of people with a common concern for accountability in their commitment. The form it takes should be determined by local realities.

Your Place in the Body Is Determined by God's Gifts to You

"From whom the whole body, joined and knit together by every joint with which it is supplied, when each part is working properly . . ." (Eph. 4:16 RSV). God's gifts to you are meant to be used, properly, in conjunction with other parts of the Body. For you to offer to serve, or to accept an invitation to serve, in a place requiring you to function outside your design may look spiritual, but it is not supported by Scripture.

That does not mean you avoid the dirty work if asked. That does not mean you cannot be put on the shelf for a while. It does not mean you do not catch somebody who is fainting because that is not your role in the Body. That is silly. That is a ploy. That avoids the central scriptural issue and admonition.

If a job to be done lacks one gifted to do it, reexamine the need for the job. God does not make mistakes. Your group may be on a man-made detour.

If you are not a leader, you do not lead. You do not lead even if you like the idea of being a leader. The leader leads because he is anointed by God to lead. He leads because leading is like breathing to him. He leads because he is designed to lead. And what is true of leading is true of teaching and administering and helping. It is true of the visible and vaunted. It is true of the hidden and lowly.

You do not announce your gift to the fellowship and create a place for yourself. As opportunities arise, you demonstrate your gift and allow the fellowship to confirm your gift and to supply increased opportunities for its use.

You Are to Be Together Frequently

"Not neglecting to meet together, as is the habit of some" (Heb. 10:25 RSV). "But exhort one another every day, as long as it is called 'today' " (Heb. 3:13 RSV). In your busy activities, you must establish priorities to lead life rather than be drowned by it. Business, family, recreation, church—is that your order of priorities?

Time is either invested or wasted. And time spent in any one area of your life is not inherently better or worse used than that spent in other areas. Much depends upon your motivation for what you do, particularly if you do what you do to delight in or please the Lord.

Aside from that important consideration, worshiping the Lord and prayer time, generating your living, and ministering to the needs of your family are probably the only time-consumers that rank higher than your active participation in the Body of Christ, of which you are a part.

Yes, Little League is of value; yes, tennis is good exercise; yes, television can occasionally be uplifting; yes, painting the counters in the church kitchen is required. Yes, spending time with the family in the evenings, just being together, not doing anything in particular, has a place in the balanced spiritual life. Yes, paperwork is necessary—sometimes. But in front of, on top of, that list and a hundred other items like it is a need critical to your spiritual health and maturity. Aside from your internal, personal life with God, active, involved participation in a body of believers is necessary to abiding in Christ—to growth, to maturity in Christ. Regardless of where your vocation has you spending your time, active membership in an active fellowship is essential.

Active involvement not only means that you meet together, but that you are also in contact with one another throughout the week. You offer to help the brethren when they need an extra hand. You ask for prayer. You pray for the brethren. You have meals together. You step into the breach when they are in trouble. You ask for help when you are in trouble, especially when you and your wife are in trouble, or you and one of your kids are having a hard time. You share wisdom. You seek wisdom.

You Are to Respect and Use One Another's Gifts

But as it is, God arranged the organs in the body, each one of them, as he chose. If all were a single organ, where would the body be? As it is, there are many parts, yet one body. The eye cannot say to the hand, "I have no need of you," nor again the head to the feet, "I have no need of you." . . . But God has so adjusted the body, giving the greater honor to the inferior part, that there may be no discord in the body, but that the members may have the same care for one another (1 Cor. 12:18–21, 24, 25 RSV).

We commit folly when we adulate the gifts of some, for example, teaching, preaching, or leading. We thereby sin and may eventually lead those we admire into sin as well. We exhibit wisdom when we seek the insight and counsel of others in the Body. Knowledge of each other's gifts, along with solicitation and active use of those gifts, is health and balance.

By themselves, our gifts can be a distortion. When mingled with other gifts, the result is a balanced diet. Social action blended with piety achieves enduring justice. Innovation tempered by prudent judgment achieves usable excellence. The big picture, when completed by someone who sees all the details, is truly worthy of praise. Penetrating judgment tempered by mercy is truth that sets free.

So we may be thrilled by the pastor's plan to win the world for Christ. But while we are so engaged, we need elder Peter's admonition about the poor in our neighborhood, elder Paul's teaching about dealing with the sin in our daily lives, and elder John's recommendation that we be faithful to give out of our income as an early step of spiritual growth.

Esteem Your Leaders for Their Work

If you have a problem with a leader (or any of the brethren), focus on the gifts God has given and the use they make of those gifts. "But we beseech you, brethren, to respect those who labor among you and are over you in the Lord and admonish you, and to esteem them very highly in love because of their work. Be at peace among yourselves" (1 Thess. 5:12, 13 RSV).

Some people we like. Some people we don't really like. Some people we feel kind of neutral about. Whatever is the case with any particular person is frequently manifested if they are in a leadership position over you.

We are commanded to give "unfeigned love" to all the brethren, including our leaders. One practical way of doing this with leaders who pose a problem to you is to look at what they are gifted in and the fruit of those gifts in your fellowship.

Do not follow the natural human tendency to justify your negative feelings by reference to a weakness. What God has given them is worthy of praise, even if the vessel has some tarnish on it in your eyes. Our Lord Jesus Himself proposed this solution for those who had a hard time accepting Him and the Father as one. "Believe me that I am in the Father and the Father in me; or else believe me for the sake of the works themselves" (John 14:11 RSV).

You Are to Submit Yourself to the Authority of the Gift Resident in Each Member

"But through love be servants of one another" (Gal. 5:13 RSV). "Be subject to one another out of reverence for Christ" (Eph. 5:21 RSV). It is to be hoped that the lay leaders effectively manifest their gifts in their secular vocations and bring the obvious authority of the gifts into the work and running of the church.

Subgroups of Those with Common Interests

"But grace was given to each of us according to the measure of Christ's gift" (Eph. 4:7 RSV). Organization of a Christian fellowship needs to include three central purposes: (1) worship, (2) growth in Jesus Christ, and (3) work in His service.

Corporate worship and general teaching and preaching have a unifying and nourishing effect on the whole church body. That is a continuing need. But the fellowship should also consider specific needs of individuals and groups within the body. Where the Christian is a babe in Christ and is beginning to work out his faith in his life, he may need fellowship with members who, apart from their leader, are similarly grappling with the compulsiveness of their motivational patterns or with habits or spiritual ignorance. The sharing, confessing, confronting, encouraging elements so critical to early growth are effective in the company of fellow beginners. In these fellowships, brethren with gifts to teach, counsel, and confront are of great value to the church.

Later, as the Christian is being equipped to function as a mature child of God, a different kind of fellowship is required, and in all probability, a different constituency. Moving from the milk of elementary doctrines of Christ earlier learned (it is hoped) from a gifted teacher and allowed to take root, the Christian needs to learn how to move in power and humility. Putting on and using the armor of Christ in his daily battle against sin and the enemy; understanding and using the spiritual gifts; understanding the mind of God in particular situations of decision and illness; and learning how to abide more often more fully—should be the items on this level of our Christian's fellowship agenda.

The mutual support of others at the same stage of the journey is as vital as the presence of experienced leaders. The point at which a person is ready to take in the meatier elements of the walk of faith does vary from one person to another. But at the right time, it is critical that the Christian move from a more introspective, sharing fellowship concerned with learning to crawl to one concerned with building spiritual muscles.

Not too soon, but at some point, the Christian needs to focus on some ministry of the church. Here the fellowship probably should include frequent meetings of those with an interest in that ministry. Although work of the local church is hardly the limits of "work in His service," we believe these ministries are foundational to the growth and character of the Kingdom on earth. Every mature Christian should contribute his gifts to one or another of such outreaches, ministering to the needy, teaching the Word of God and so on. For example, teachers should teach, salespeople and influencers should evangelize, helpers should distribute food and services to the poor, and counselors should work with widows and troubled teens and couples.

Humility is not denying your strengths it is... Rather know your weaknesses

You Are to Confess Your Strengths to One Another

"Therefore confess your sins to one another, and pray for one another, that you may be healed" (James 5:16 RSV). "Bear one another's burdens, and so fulfill the law of Christ" (Gal. 6:2 RSV). Among those trespasses we usually think of as sin, there are those that lie close to our strengths. For that reason, sin is frequently traceable to misuse of, overuse of, or failure to use our gifts. We need to understand the motivational pattern of each member of the Body.

For example, the gift of perfecting and mastering can be abused by throttling ideas that do not lend themselves to perfecting. Both the perfectionist and the Body need to be aware of the gift and its potential abuse, and to seek the cleansing of confession and forgiveness when harm has been done in compulsively following it.

Another example would be the person who is so motivated to please and serve others that she is unable to speak the truth she perceives, afraid that she may offend. She needs to confess.

A further example is the person with the gift of discernment who uses it to be critical or to be depressed. Confession of those propensities and prayer by the Body to be healed of the misuse are in order.

You Are to "Deal" with One Another's Pattern

"Let the word of Christ dwell in you richly, as you teach and admonish one another in all wisdom" (Col. 3:16 RSV). "Therefore, putting away falsehood, let every one speak the truth with his neighbor, for we are members one of another" (Eph. 4:25 RSV). As painful as it is for some, as enjoyable as it is for others, all of us need to admonish and to be admonished at one time or another. The Lord uses other people to discipline us, to reprove, to chastise us. A reading of Hebrews 12:1–13 will make that clear. Discipline is a sign He loves us. It is a sign that the brethren love one another, for truth of a difficult sort can require naked, unfeigned love to motivate its delivery. When you are on the receiving end of that love, the spanking does the job, but it never wounds the spirit.

Moving ahead of the Lord to do our thing; using some tenuous excuse to justify doing what we want to do; grabbing any pretense to direct attention to ourselves; thrusting out of the Spirit into the domain of rancorous debate to prove I am right; justifying my overcontrol of a situation; failing to do necessary detail work in my area of responsiiblity because I am too busy doing "important" tasks; and a hundred similar moves—all need attention by others in the Body.

Finally, a most important point about Christian discipline: We question whether any one person can discipline another person in all areas of his life. The Scripture says we are subject to one another, and that means there is no one authority over all matters except Jesus Christ. No one person has more than a few gifts from God. Any person who moves beyond his anointed gifts and presumes to act in an authoritative way is moving without God's clear sanction.

You Are Not to Murmur against One Another

Do not speak evil against one another, brethren (James 4:11 RSV).

Do not grumble, brethren, against one another (James 5:9 RSV).

May the God of steadfastness and encouragement grant you to live in such harmony with one another, in accord with Christ Jesus, that together you may with one voice glorify the God and Father of our Lord Jesus Christ (Rom. 15:5, 6 RSV).

I appeal to you, brethren, by the name of our Lord Jesus Christ, that all of you agree and that there be no dissensions among you, but that you be united in the same mind and the same judgment (1 Cor. 1:10 RSV).

But if you bite and devour one another take heed that you are not consumed by one another (Gal. 5:15 RSV).

Let us have no self-conceit, no provoking of one another, no envy of one another (Gal. 5:26).

In spite of how dumb, indolent, blind, pigheaded, talkative, fleshly, superspiritual, artsy, slovenly, phony, humble-humble, theoretical, controlling, or hypocritical you perceive your brethren to be, we have no choice. If we begin to carp, we begin to destroy. If we begin to criticize, we start a long, accelerating slide into hardness of heart that, taken collectively, will kill the Body.

There is no justification for a critical spirit. It does not edify anyone to be continually exposed to a finely honed talent to perceive and announce what is wrong. We cannot recall many instances where anybody benefited from even enlightened murmuring.

One way to reduce critical responses to others is to understand the motivational patterns of the members of your Body. When we know their actions stem from their gifts and motivations, we can feel differently in the middle of a collision of what was seen as personality clashes. Charlie seeks to control, Harriet to encourage, Stan to impress, Mary to minister, John to innovate, Bob to engineer, Roberta to teach. Knowing each pattern, you can better accept what comes with the people behind the patterns. We are then less inclined to take what is said personally. We are less inclined to condemn, because what the other person says and does makes obvious sense in his eyes. We are much more inclined to enjoy one another, or at least to be understanding and charitable.

You Are to Have Unfeigned Love for the Brethren

"Seeing ye have purified your souls in obeying the truth through the Spirit unto unfeigned love of the brethren, see that ye love one another with a pure heart fervently" (1 Pet. 1:22 KJV). To reach a point of unfeigned love for others, we must first open ourselves to such love from God. Only when we have experienced the reality of such passion and have seen the enormity of our sin and His sacrifice for us do we begin to understand what the Lord has commanded us to give one another.

In terms of gifts through which we love, the admonition for fervent, unfeigned love contemplates an unconditional giving of our gifts, ready availability to others in the Body, and active pursuit of those loved ones if the relationship is threatened. Such love is the antithesis of the social rules we normally follow.

If one member is in trouble in any area of his life, someone goes to that person and gets involved. If a member starts walking away from the Body or closes up meaningful communication, someone moves and finds out why, and the confessions and prayer start flowing.

God's love is strong in tearing down what stands in its way. God commands us to love His way, and He has provided the power to do so, if we will.

You Are to Love through Your Gifts

Above all, keep your love for one another at full strength, because love cancels innumerable sins. Be hospitable to one another without complaining. Whatever gift each of you may have received, use it in service to one another, like good stewards dispensing the grace of God in its varied forms (1 Pet. 4:8–10 NEB).

Perhaps I am not gifted at counseling, but I can grow a beautiful garden. I am not gifted at teaching the gospel, but I can make handsome benches. I am not gifted at visiting the sick and making them feel better, but I am good at baking pies to take to others. I am not good at welcoming people and engaging them in conversation, but I am gifted at fixing things broken by their kids.

Come see the wonderful photograph I made of a barren tree. Would you come over for dinner next Wednesday night? Doesn't she handle those tough kids well? Harry is such a solid rock, you can always trust what he says.

We love mainly through the gifts God has given us, to be poured out for others. I give you myself through my music. I give you love through my defending an unpopular member, through the extra money I give, through my encouragement, through my listening, through being who I was created to be.

You Are to Encourage and Build Up One Another

"Let us consider how to stir up one another to love and good works" (Heb. 10:24 RSV). "But exhort one another every day" (Heb. 3:13 RSV). "Therefore encourage one another and build one another up, just as you are doing" (1 Thess. 5:11 RSV). Certain of the brethren need much encouragement and building up. They need the fellowship to encourage them to use their gifts and contributions without fear of judgment. That would be true, for example, of people who have only used their gifts in hobbies where they weren't paid for them, or who are tentatively considering a career change at age thirty-five.

The new Christian has his pattern encumbered by all sorts of clutter. Being freed up in the proper sense requires a cradle of understanding and love. For example, the fellowship needs to encourage those who say,

"I believe I have a really great idea that will help the company I work for, but I am afraid people will laugh at me."

"I really would like to go to school and learn how to compose music, but how many people make a living writing songs?"

"Starting a gas station of my own has always been a dream of mine, but Harriet is worried about losing my medical benefits."

"My husband says my place is in the home, but with the kids grown, I really want to sell real estate."

To the person needing help, encouragement and support are vital to a good foundation, so one of the major ministries of the church body is to edify and encourage each member. Many Christians are unsure how to do this. For some of them, giving and receiving praise seems to come close to encouraging sin. Here are some practical suggestions.

How to Give Praise

Talk about, praise, point to, and approve the *work*, not the person. Say, for example, ''That teaching was so clear to me. Thank you so much.'' Do not say, ''You are such a fine teacher.'' Or say, ''I enjoy so much the way you arrange flowers. Thank you for doing such a fine job.'' Don't say, ''You are such a good flower arranger.''

In this way, we draw attention to the gift God has given, affirm its exercise, and edify without drawing attention necessarily to the person who otherwise has to go through theological gymnastics deciding whether he or God is supposed to get the credit. Also, one need not limit compliments about the work at all, whereas praise for the performer must have its limitations.

Technique for Receiving Praise

''You are such a fine teacher,'' someone says. Respond, ''Thank you so much, I surely do enjoy the subject.'' Do not say, ''Well, it wasn't me. It was the Lord.'' Or someone says, ''You are such a good singer.'' Respond ''Thanks so much, I'm glad it was a blessing to you.'' Don't say, ''Oh, I can't sing that well.''

We can draw attention to the work or to the results that everyone knows are only possible because of God's gift without having to give a spontaneous teaching on the subject. Nor does the Lord need to be given total responsibility for your singing, since that embraces your vocal flaws as well as your excellence. We have often heard second-rate Christian composers say ''God gave me this song,'' and they then proceed to sing a song that might have been a blessing to some, but that by any reasonable standards of good music was evidence of appalling musical taste on the part of God.

We know God is the originator of our gifts, but we must recognize that since redemption is *still* being worked out in our faculties, minds, and bodies, by the time the gift works its way through, a bit of the initial luster may be missing.

You Are to Serve the World through Your Gifts

Those who have come to believe in God should see that they engage in honourable occupations, which are not only honourable in themselves, but also useful to their fellow-men (Titus 3:8 NEB).

And our own people must be taught to engage in honest employment to produce the necessities of life; they must not be unproductive (Titus 3:14 NEB).

Labor of its members in vocations that produce good and useful services to mankind is an essential accompaniment to mature functioning of the Body of Christ. Only a very few spend their lives working full-time for the church. Most of us spend the bulk of our lives in the world, serving the world with God's gifts.

The Body to which we belong should be able to help us gird our loins to go into battle and nurse our wounds as we return. This is perhaps the most important function of the Body, that is, to train and equip its members to be lights in their worlds.

The Body can get into trouble by failing to embrace the gifts of its members when the exercise of those gifts occurs mainly in the world. If I am a lawyer, a merchant, a dentist, a farmer, or a machinist with gifts appropriate to those vocations, the Body makes my life of work irrelevant to my life of faith unless it includes all of me when we are together. Unless it learns about the details of my work, my problems, my anxieties, and my irritations in using my gifts in my work life, the Body cannot effectively provide any support in a meaningful way. It cannot encourage me where I need encouragement, confront me when I need it, or quiet me when I have unreasonable fear.

When the Body gathers, most of what it deals with, after worshiping the Lord, should emanate from the real-life circumstances and concerns of its members. Consider praying for, doing battle with, encouraging, admonishing, seeking the mind of the Lord—about a business decision, a new design, a difficult boss or customer, a job change, a schedule slippage, a critical test, an unfair competition, or an obnoxious teacher.

Those are sometimes more needful than more obviously "spiritual" concerns, and being concrete, they can be realistic tests of our prayer effectiveness.

We dare to suggest a further level of commitment. Why shouldn't the Body contribute out of its financial resources to provide security during a career change for one of its members? Why not enable a brother or sister to set aside time to take on a job campaign without worry about family, by providing funds, meals, babysitting, and encouragement? Why shouldn't the goal-setting, organizing, planning, and counseling gifts in the Body be applied to job-misfit situations and to enabling young people to make good career choices? Why not have the Body become a living witness to the world that the Christian faith embraces all of life and Christian love accompanies each member to his place in the world of work, that nothing is outside God's grace?

14

Where It Is All Headed

THE MOST INESCAPABLE FACT OF MORTAL LIFE is that it ends. It ends in spite of the fact that it seems unnatural for human life to end. The Resurrection is the door to eternity, where we will come into an unhampered use of our gifts in a kingdom in which everyone will be able to fully express his gifts without the labor that accompanied them on earth. " 'Blessed are the dead who die in the Lord henceforth.' 'Blessed indeed,' says the Spirit, 'that they may rest from their labors, for their deeds follow them!' " (Rev. 14:13 RSV). That verse assures us of rest and goes on to state that our work on earth will follow us into eternity. What we do here that endures God's judgment will be with us.

Whatever form our works will take in eternity, whether character, knowledge, approbation, or glory, it is comforting to know that what we do in time with our lives has eternal consequence.

There is a sobering process between time and eternity, however, called judgment. It is mentioned frequently in the Bible as a warning to man to pay attention to what he is doing.

I the LORD search the mind and try the heart, to give to every man according to his ways, according to the fruit of his doings (Jer. 17:10 RSV).

And that to thee, O Lord, belongs steadfast love. For thou dost requite a man according to his work (Psalm 62:12 RSV).

And I saw the dead, great and small, standing before the throne, and books were opened. Also another book was opened, which is the book of life. And the dead were judged by what was written in the books, by what they had done. And the sea gave up the dead in it, Death and Hades gave up the dead in them, and all were judged by what they had done (Rev. 20:12, 13 RSV).

Behold, I am coming soon, bringing my recompense, to repay every one for what he has done (Rev. 22:12 RSV).

Each man's work will become manifest; for the Day will disclose it, because it will be revealed with fire, and the fire will test what sort of work each one has done. If the work which any man has built on the foundation survives, he will receive a reward (1 Cor. 3:13, 14 RSV).

We know when we have Jesus as Lord that our salvation is assured. But Scripture insists, through the preceding verses and especially in the parable of the talents (Matt. 25:14–30), that there will be a difference between one believer and another.

That difference is expressed in terms of rewards. Rewards in time are passing, but in eternity they are forever. That alone magnifies the meaning of the "Well done, good and faithful servant" of Matthew 25:21.

There is to be eternal praise from God for the faithful Christian. We look forward to His "Well done," and we will live for eternity in the pleasure of His being pleased. Our being able to respond properly will come from lessons learned here. We will remember the experiences we had when others responded to some good we accomplished and we had (perhaps fleetingly) the flush of pleasure in that affirmation of our work—the sense of our worthiness coming from parents, friends, and fellow workers. In spite of all the perversion in pride and lust for fame or recognition, there still is the possibility of a wholesome "Well done" that is good and God-pleasing.

Originally self-lovers, our attempt at happiness was once to exploit all praise in order to affirm our self-centeredness and use it to prove our worth. It was a sick self telling itself its worth.

Then God made it possible for our slavish passion for ourselves to be replaced by a free, natural love for Him. Our work became a demonstration of our love for Him. Now our purposes for work and the quality of our work are all for Him, but for One we have yet to see face to face. Enjoying the response of others is seen in the light of God's ultimate response.

Suddenly God breaks through the distance and we realize that God is the audience for all the work we have done. He is the judge of its worth. But its worth is not isolated within utilitarian purposes in time. Its worth is in its truth as a language of love. We can say, whatever the work, "I did it for You," and discover the response "Well done, good and faithful servant."

What will it be like for the Author of the universe to so bless us?

Surely that reward is worth the risk of worshiping God by following His plan for our lives.

Brethren, I do not consider that I have made it my own; but one thing I do, forgetting what lies behind and straining forward to what lies ahead, I press on toward the goal for the prize of the upward call of God in Christ Jesus (Phil. 3:13, 14 RSV).

Appendix

System for Identifying Motivated Abilities*

Biographical Information

IF YOU ARE LIKE MOST PEOPLE, YOU HAVE NEVer taken time to sort out the things you are good at and motivated to accomplish. As a result, it is unlikely that you use these talents as completely or effectively as you could.

Identification of your strengths and vocationally significant motivations is the purpose of SIMA.

To complete this form, you are asked to list and describe things you have done that you: (1) enjoyed doing and (2) believed you did well.

Such achievement experiences may have occurred in your work or your home life or your leisure time.

It is imperative that you put down what was important to you. Do not put down what you believe other people might think as important. Also, it is essential that you relate specific achievement experiences and not general ones. To help you understand the type of achievement experiences we are after, you will find, following, examples of things other people have listed as personally significant.

There is no time limit to complete the form. IT IS NOT A TEST, so enjoy yourself. There are no right or wrong answers.

Summary Examples

"Putting on plays for neighborhood children with costumes,

*SIMA Biographical Form, People Management, Inc. Simsbury, Connecticut 06070 © 1980.

props, etc. The most successful project was transforming a shed in back of our house into a fairyland with lighting effects, decorations, princesses, witches, etc."

"I built and mastered the tallest pair of stilts in my neighborhood. I started a stilt craze among my friends."

"I had a job as a printer's devil. I developed a method of cutting stereotypes which was faster and more accurate than that previously used."

"I established an evening routine of a quiet time of sharing and reading with our children which made bedtime an enjoyable end to the day."

"Was a prime mover in starting company. Saw utility of product concept. Had much to do with early market development. Helped conceive basic manufacturing concepts."

"Organized and ran a company-sponsored national conference with about 100 participants. Conference was a resounding success."

Personal Achievements, Not Experiences

In describing your achievements, remember that although an achievement may refer to leisure time experiences or to impressions, personal observations or other intangible feelings, relationships, etc., the achievement must be something you not only experienced, but centrally it must be something you achieved, something you enjoyed doing and believed you did well.

You need to provide details of something you did specifically. For example:

Not good: "Had a great time on my trip to Europe."

Good: "Came to understand European culture on my trip to Europe."

Also good: "Took some stunning photos on my trip to Europe."

Finally, don't feel you have to cover every year in your life. This is not an autobiographical account of your whole life, but rather a look at the highlights.

Summary Achievements

For each period, briefly describe two or more specific things you accomplished that you enjoyed doing and believed you did well. If it would be helpful, put the calendar years covered under the age period; i.e. " '49–'53"—create additional categories for more achievements if you wish to add (a-3, b-3, etc.).

Childhood
(a-1)   Solicited business to mow lawns in the neighborh I live in. Enjoyed it and made more, to buy Christmas gifts for my family)

(a-2)   Enter my dog "Tommy" in a Dog show. Trained for the event and got Pleasure from doing it.

(a-3)   Delivered Papers in our Neighbourhs, (Won Contest ie Hotel Room with my Brother)

Teen Years
(If you are in this age group, continue listing examples, ignoring the age categories which follow. List as many examples as you can remember.)
(b-1)

(b-2)

Age 18-22
(c-1)

(c-2)

Age _____
(d-1)

(d-2)

Age _____
(e-1)

(e-2)

Age _____
(f-1)

(f-2)

Age _____
(g-1)

(g-2)

Age _____
(h-1)

(h-2)

Of the things you have described, note in the boxes below the eight most important to you (e.g. b-2, f-1), not necessarily in order of importance. Please place an asterisk* next to the summary achievements (above) you have chosen.

Expanding on the Most Important Achievements

Taking the eight most important achievements in the order given in the preceding boxes, describe:

1. How you got involved in it;

2. The details of what you actually did (elaborate and expand); and,

3. What was particularly enjoyable or satisfying to you.

Some individuals like to write, so will thoroughly enjoy this exercise. Others are reluctant to do this much writing. If you are in the latter category, you might dictate your expansion into a tape recorder and have someone transcribe your words onto the following pages.

Try to fill each page, focusing on the details of what you actually did.

Start each page by repeating the summary statement about the achievement.

Achievement (   ) 1

   One line summary statement:

   How you got involved:

   Details of what you did (how you actually went about doing
it):

Achievement (   ) 2

One line summary statement:

How you got involved:

Details of what you did (how you actually went about doing it):

What was particularly satisfying to you:

Achievement (   ) 3

One line summary statement:

How you got involved:

Details of what you did (how you actually went about doing it):

What was particularly satisfying to you:

Achievement (   ) 4

One line summary statement:

How you got involved:

Details of what you did (how you actually went about doing it):

What was particularly satisfying to you:

Achievement (   ) 5

One line summary statement:

How you got involved:

Details of what you did (how you actually went about doing it):

What was particularly satisfying to you:

Achievement (   ) 6

One line summary statement:

How you got involved:

Details of what you did (how you actually went about doing
it):

What was particularly satisfying to you:

Achievement (   ) 7

One line summary statement:

How you got involved:

Details of what you did (how you actually went about doing it):

What was particularly satisfying to you:

Achievement (   ) 8

One line summary statement:

How you got involved:

Details of what you did (how you actually went about doing it):

What was particularly satisfying to you:

Work Chronology

Dates	Organization	Title-Function

EDUCATION SUMMARY

College - Year - Degree - Major

Graduate Work

Activities

Favorite Subjects - College   H.S.

SPARE TIME INFORMATION

What activities give you most pleasure outside of work?

When you were a child?